FOREIGN EXCHANGE AND MANAGEMENT ACT- SUPREME COURT'S LEADING CASE LAWS

CASE NOTES- FACTS- FINDINGS OF APEX COURT JUDGES & CITATIONS

JAYPRAKASH BANSILAL SOMANI

ISBN 979-888591706-3

Dedicated

To

All the Past & Present Judges of the Supreme Court of India.

Salute to their wisdom.

Salute to their interpretation of Law.

Salute to their elaborative judgement writing.

Contents

Contents

Preface

Dear Learned Advocates of the Trial Courts, Tribunals, High Courts, Supreme Court, Corporates, Chartered Accountants & Individuals

I am very delighted to provide you a book on 'FOREIGN EXCHANGE AND MANAGEMENT ACT'- Supreme Court of India's Leading Case Laws'.

In this book you will get...

1. Name of the Case i. e. Cause title

2.Relevant Sections discussed in the case

3. Hon'ble Judges/Coram of the case

4.Number of PDF Pages in Original Judgement of the case

5. All available Citations of the case

6. Case Note with appeal allowed/ dismissed or disposed off

7. Facts of the case

8. Hon'ble Apex Court's findings, while dismissing/allowing or disposing the appeal

9. Ratio Decidendi if any.

My special thanks to Manupatra, because of their web portal I can compile this book in well manner. I am also thankful to Notion Press to support me to publish & market this book throughout the Country. Thanks to my Juniors, Advocate Colleagues & Insolvency Professional Colleagues to support me in this venture.

Mr Rachit Manchanda has helped me a lot to compile this book.

I hope this book will add some value addition in the wealth of your legal knowledge. Your positive feedbacks will boost me to compile/ write further books & negative feedbacks will improve my skills. Kindly send your valuable feedbacks by email.

Thanks with Regards,

Jayprakash B. Somani

Advocate, Supreme Court of India

Email: jaysomani64@gmail.com

Web Site:www.jayprakashsomani.com

Call: 8384051134, 9322188701, 9318381287

Acknowledgements

Printed & Published by
Notion Press
No. 8, 3rd Cross Street,
CIT Colony, Mylapore,
Chennai, Tamil Nadu- 600004

ÞÞÞ

Managed by
Jayprakash Somani Advocates & Solicitors
Law Firm for Supreme Court of India
Delhi Office
257 C, Pocket 1, Mayur Vihar Phase 1, Delhi 110091.
Call 8384051134, 9322188701, 8459194576, 9318381287 01141051516
Supreme Court Chamber
312, 3rd Floor, M. C. Setalvad Block, In front of 'D' Gate, Bhagwan Das Road, Supreme Court of India, New Delhi 110001
Contact: 8459194576, 9811011747,
www.jayprakashsomani.com

ÞÞÞ

Books are available online at
1. Notion Press: https://notionpress.com/author/jayprakash_somani
2. Amazon: https://www.amazon.in/s?k=jayprakash+somani
3. Flipkart: https://www.flipkart.com/search?q=Jayprakash%20Somani

ÞÞÞ

ONE

SUBORNO BOSE VS. ENFORCEMENT DIRECTORATE AND ORS., 2020

Hon'ble Judges/Coram: A.M. Khanwilkar and Dinesh Maheshwari, JJ.

Relevant Section:

Foreign Exchange Management Act, 1999 - Section 42(1)

Equivalent Citation: AIR2020SC4288, [2020]159CLA1(SC), 2020(372)ELT3(S.C.), (2020)2MLJ646, (2020)14SCC241, [2020]160SCL607(SC), MANU/SC/0285/2020

No. of pages in the Original Judgement: 7

Case Note:

FEMA - Penalty - Determination of liability - Sections 10(6), 42(1), 46 and 47 of Foreign Exchange Management Act, 1999 - Show cause notice was issued to Appellant, stating that Adjudicating Authority was satisfied that there was prima facie contravention of Section 10(6) of FEMA Act read with Sections 46 and 47 of said Act - Reply to show-cause notice filed on behalf of Company including for Appellant - Adjudicating Authority concluded that noticee Company and Appellant had violated Section 10(6) of FEMA Act read with Sections 46 and 47 of Act having found that goods had arrived in India, but Company failed to submit Bill of Entry and did not take delivery of goods - Resultantly, Adjudicating Authority imposed penalty on Appellant and noticee company - Company, as well as, Appellant filed appeals before

Appellate authority - Appellate Authority dismissed appeals and was pleased to uphold decision of Adjudicating Authority - Being aggrieved, Company, as well as Appellant carried matter before High Court - Both appeals were dismissed by High Court - Hence, present appeal - Whether Appellant could be made liable for contravention committed by erstwhile management of Company.

Brief Facts of the case:

A show-cause notice was issued to the Appellant, stating that the Adjudicating Authority was satisfied that there was a prima facie contravention of Section 10(6) of the FEMA Act read with Sections 46 and 47 of the said Act and the Foreign Exchange Manual in the complaint filed against the company of which, the Appellant was the Managing Director. The reply to the show-cause notice filed on behalf of the Company including for the Appellant and the submissions made before the Adjudicating Authority were duly considered by the Adjudicating Authority. The Adjudicating Authority concluded that the noticee Company and the Appellant had violated the provisions of Section 10(6) of the FEMA Act read with Sections 46 and 47 of the said Act read with the Foreign Exchange Manual having found that the goods had arrived in India, but the Company failed to submit Bill of Entry and did not take delivery of the goods. The import formalities would have had completed only after submission of Bill of Entry. Thus, though the goods for which foreign exchange was remitted had reached the destination of the users, but the same were not released and as such kept in bonded warehouse. That resulted in contravention warranting issuance of show-cause notice to the Company and the Appellant. Resultantly, the Adjudicating Authority imposed penalty on Appellant and the company. The Company, as well as, the Appellant carried the matter in appeal before the Special Director (Appeals), FEMA and Commissioner of Income-Tax. The Appellate Authority dismissed both the appeals and was pleased to uphold the decision of the Adjudicating Authority. Being aggrieved, the Company, as well as the Appellant carried the matter before the High Court. Both appeals were dismissed by the High Court.

Held,

The Tribunal has erroneously relied on the judgment in *Hindustan Steel Ltd. v. State of Orissa*, MANU/SC/0418/1969 : (1969) 2 SCC 627 which pertained to criminal/quasi-criminal proceedings. That Section 25 of the Orissa Sales Tax Act which was in question in the said case imposed a punishment of imprisonment up to six months and fine for the offences under the Act. The said case has no application in the present case which relates to imposition of civil liabilities under the SEBI Act and the Regulations and is not a criminal/quasi-criminal proceeding.

We are in agreement with the view so expressed.

To sum up, we hold that no error has been committed by the adjudicating authority in finding that the Appellant was also liable to be proceeded with for the contravention by the Company of which he became the Managing Director and for penalty therefor as prescribed for the contravention of Section 10(6) read with Sections 46 and 47 of the FEMA Act read with paragraphs A-10 and A-11 (Current Account Transaction) of the Foreign Exchange Manual 2003-04. The first appellate authority and the High Court justly affirmed the view so taken by the adjudicating authority.

Accordingly, this appeal fails and the same is dismissed with no order as to costs.

PPP

TWO

UNION OF INDIA (UOI) AND ORS. VS. PREMIER LIMITED AND ORS., 2019

Hon'ble Judges/Coram: Abhay Manohar Sapre and Indira Banerjee, JJ.

Relevant Section:

Foreign Exchange Regulation Act, 1973 - Section 50; Section 51, Section 52, Section 54, Section 81; Section 17, Section 18, Section 19, Section 49

Equivalent Citation: 2019(2)ALLMR939, 2019(2)BomCR860, [2019]150CLA1(SC), [2019]213CompCas1(SC), 2019(365)ELT657(S.C.), 2019(3)KarLJ418, (2019)2MLJ483, 2019(2)SCALE373, (2020)14SCC492, 2019 (5) SCJ 118, [2019]152SCL226(SC), MANU/SC/0094/2019

No. of pages in the Original Judgement: 9

Case Note:

FERA - Jurisdiction - Present appeal was filed by Union of India against final judgment of High Court holding that, appeals filed by Respondent Nos. 2 to 4 before Special Director (Appeals) against adjudication order were maintainable as Special Director (Appeals) possessed jurisdiction to decide appeals on merits - if Adjudicating Officer had passed an order after repeal of FERA in proceedings initiated prior to 1st June, 2000, whether an appeal against such order would lie before "Special Director (Appeals)" under Section 17 of FEMA or before "Appellate Tribunal" under Section 19 of FEMA.

Brief facts of the case:

On 1st May, 1991, a memorandum to show cause notice was issued by Special Director to Respondent Nos. 2, 3 and 4, namely, M/s. Godrej Industries Ltd. [formerly known as Godrej Soaps Ltd. (R-2)] and its two Directors (R-3 and R-4) for allegedly committing contravention of Sections 9 (1) (a), 9(1)(c) and Section 16(1) of Foreign Exchange Regulation Act, 1973 (hereinafter referred to as "FERA") in respect of imports and exports of certain commodities made with two foreign parties, viz., M/s. Fingrain, S.A., Geneva and M/s. Continental Grain Export Corporation, New York during the year 1977-78. During pendency of proceedings, FERA was repealed with effect from 1st June, 2000. It was, however, replaced by Foreign Exchange Management Act, 1999 ("FEMA"). On 5th December, 2003, an adjudication order was passed by Deputy Director of Enforcement under FEMA read with FERA in relation to show cause notice dated 1st May, 1991. By this order, penalty of Rs. 15,50,000 was imposed on M/s. Godrej Industries Ltd. and its two Directors for contravening the provisions of Sections 9 (1)(a) and 9(1)(c) read with Section 16 (1) of FERA. On 15th January, 2004, Respondent Nos. 2 to 4 felt aggrieved by adjudication order dated 5th December, 2003 and filed appeal before Special Director (Appeals) under Section 17 of FEMA. Special Director (Appeals) dismissed appeals as being not maintainable holding that, Special Director (Appeals) had no jurisdiction to hear appeals against adjudication order passed under Section 51 of FERA. Respondent Nos. 2 to 4 felt aggrieved by orders and filed writ petitions before High Court. By impugned common order, High Court allowed writ petitions and quashed orders of Special Director (Appeals). High Court held that, appeals filed by Respondent Nos. 2 to 4 before Special Director (Appeals) against adjudication order were maintainable as Special Director (Appeals) possessed jurisdiction to decide appeals on merits. It was against this order of High Court, Revenue had felt aggrieved and filed present appeal by way of special leave before present Court.

Held,

The anomalous situation would be, the orders passed by the Appellate Tribunal in the appeals, which stood transferred to the Appellate Tribunal by virtue of Section 49 (5)(b), are appealable to the High Court Under Section 35 of FEMA whereas the orders passed by the Special Director (Appeals) in the appeals filed after 01.06.2000 are not appealable to the High Court Under Section 35 of FEMA. So, against the same order, one Appellant has a right of appeal to the High Court but the other Appellant has no such right of appeal because he suffered dismissal of his appeal from Special Director (Appeals) against whose order appeal does not lie Under Section 35 to the High Court. In our view, such anomalous situation while interpreting the provisions of the Act should always be avoided.

Applying the principle of purposive interpretation, we are of the view that the appellate forum for deciding the appeals arising out of the order passed Under Section 51 of FERA whether filed prior to 01.06.2000 or filed after 01.06.2000 must be the same, i.e., Appellate Tribunal under FEMA.

In view of the foregoing discussion, we cannot concur with the view taken by the High Court and accordingly hold that the appeal filed by Respondent Nos. 2 to 4 against the order dated 05.12.2003 passed by Deputy Director of enforcement Under Section 51 of FERA will lie and was, therefore, maintainable only before the Appellate Tribunal Under Section 19 of FEMA.

The appeals bearing Nos. SD/A/MUM/04-05/38,39,40 and SD/A/MUM/03-04/22 which Respondent Nos. 2 to 4 had filed before the Special Director (Appeals) are accordingly transferred to the concerned Appellate Tribunal constituted Under Section 18 of FEMA for their disposal on merits in accordance with law.

The appeal is accordingly allowed. The impugned order is set aside.

THREE

Maars Software International Ltd. and Ors. Vs. Union of India (UOI) and Ors., 2019

Hon'ble Judges/Coram: Abhay Manohar Sapre and Dinesh Maheshwari, JJ.

Acts/Rules/Orders:

Foreign Exchange Management Act, 1999 - Section 8, Section 13, Section 16(3), Section 35, Section 42, Section 42(1); Foreign Exchange Management (Realization, Repatriation and Surrender of Foreign Exchange) Regulations, 2000 - Regulation 3, Regulation 9

Equivalent Citation: AIR2019SC2849, [2019]214CompCas485(SC), (2020)1CompLJ473(SC), 2019(366)ELT598(S.C.), 2019(6)SCALE570, (2019)11SCC291, [2019]153SCL385(SC), MANU/SC/0579/2019

No. of pages in the Original Judgement: 3

Case Note:

FEMA - Violation of provision - Validity of complaint - Enforcement Directorate filed complaint, against Appellant-Company before Special Director of Enforcement - Complaint was found on material collected during course of investigation made in affairs and dealings of Appellant-Company in their business operations - Special Director allowed complaint and held that Appellant-Company had contravened provisions of FEMA and imposed penalty - On appeal, Tribunal set aside order of Special Director - On further appeal, High Court set aside order of Tribunal and restored order of Adjudicating Authority - Hence, present appeal - Whether High Court erred in setting aside order of Tribunal relating to validity of complaint.

Brief facts of the case:

The Enforcement Directorate filed a complaint, under Section 16 (3) of the Foreign Exchange Management Act, 1999 against the Appellant-Company before the Special Director of Enforcement (Adjudicating Authority). The complaint was founded on the material collected during the course of detailed investigation made in the affairs and the dealings of the Appellant-Company in their business operations. The Special Director allowed the complaint and held that the Appellant-Company had contravened the provisions of FEMA and accordingly imposed a penalty. On appeal, the Tribunal set aside the order and directed the authorities to refund the amount which was deposited by the Appellants in these proceedings for filing the appeals. On further appeal, the High Court allowed the appeals, set aside the order of the Tribunal and restored the order of the Adjudicating Authority.

Held, while allowing the appeal: (i) The Appellants had filed material, in the case, with a view to show as to what steps they had taken to realize and repatriate the dues in question.

(ii) It was clear that the High Court did not examine the case of the parties in the context of material placed by the Appellants.

Held,

In our considered view, keeping in view the observations made by the High Court in Para 15, it is clear that the High Court did not examine the case of the parties in the context of material placed by the Appellants, though the Tribunal in Para 29 of its order has considered the said material.

In our view, the High Court should have taken into consideration the said material with a view to decide as to whether it was relevant or/and sufficient, and whether it could justify the Appellants' case as contemplated Under Section 8 of FEMA.

Instead, the High Court seemed to have proceeded on wrong assumption that since the Appellants did not file any material, a case was made out against them. This observation of the High Court, in our view, was contrary to the record of the case and hence, interference in the impugned order is called for.

In view of the foregoing discussion, we are of the view that the proper course in such a case would be to remand the case to the High Court and request the High Court to decide the appeal afresh on merits in accordance with law.

In view of the foregoing discussion, the appeals succeed and are accordingly allowed. The impugned order is set aside. The case is remanded to the High Court for deciding the appeals afresh on merits in accordance with law keeping in view the observations made above.

We, however, make it clear that we have not expressed any opinion on the merits of the controversy having formed an opinion to remand the case to the High Court on the grounds mentioned above.

The High Court will decide the appeals uninfluenced by any observation made in the impugned order and in this order.

FOUR

THIRUMALAI CHEMICALS LIMITED VS. UNION OF INDIA (UOI) AND ORS., 2011

Hon'ble Judges/Coram: R.V. Raveendran and K.S. Panicker Radhakrishnan, JJ.

Relevant Section:

Foreign Exchange Management Act, 1999 - Section 49; Section 8; Section 13, Section 19

Equivalent Citation: 2011(101)AIC53, AIR2011SC1725, 2011 5 AWC4585SC, 2012(1)BomCR790, [2011]102CLA269(SC), [2011]163CompCas380(SC), (2011)3CompLJ46(SC), (2011)3CompLJ46(SC), 2011(268)ELT296(S.C.), JT2011(4)SC453, 2011(4)KCCRSN395, 2011(3)RCR(Civil)20, 2011(4)SCALE642, (2011)6SCC739, [2011]108SCL78(SC), [2011]4SCR838, 2011(2)UJ1670, MANU/SC/0427/2011

No. of pages in the Original Judgement: 7

Case Note:

FEMA - Delay - Section 19 of the Foreign Exchange Management Act, 1999(FEMA) - Appellate Tribunal constituted under FEMA rejected belated appeal filed under Section 19 of FEMA - Hence the Appeal - Whether Appellate Tribunal constituted under the FEMA was right in rejecting a belated appeal filed under Section 19 of FEMA, applying first proviso to Section 52(2) of FERA, instead of following proviso to Section 19(2) of FEMA -

Held, Section 49 of FEMA did not seek to withdraw or take away vested right of appeal in cases where proceedings were initiated prior to repeal of FERA on 1st June, 2000 or after – Procedure prescribed by FEMA only would be applicable in respect of an appeal filed under FEMA though cause of action arose under FERA - Findings rendered by Courts below that Tribunal did not have jurisdiction to condone delay beyond date prescribed under FERA was not correct understanding of law on the subject -Appellate Tribunal can entertain appeal after prescribed period of 45 days if it satisfied, that there was sufficient cause for not filing the appeal within the said period - Court set aside impugned judgments - Remitted matter back to Tribunal for fresh consideration in accordance with law - Appeal Disposed of.

Ratio Decidendi:

"Procedure prescribed by FEMA only would be applicable in respect of anappeal filed under FEMA, though cause of action arose under FERA."

Brief Facts of the case:

The question that has come up for consideration in this case is whether the Appellate Tribunal constituted under the Foreign Exchange Management Act 1999 (in short FEMA) was right in rejecting a belated appeal filed under Section 19 of FEMA, applying the first proviso to Sub-section (2) of Section 52 of Foreign Exchange Regulation Act 1973 (in short FERA), instead of following the proviso to Sub-section (2) to Section 19 of FEMA.

M/s Tirumalai Chemicals Limited (in short 'the Company') had imported various consignments of benezene, orthoxalene etc. for home consumption. For the said purpose, the Company had opened Letters of Credit bearing No. MLCO 4359096 and No. 529/960487 on 28.09.96 and 07.08.96 respectively on their bankers ICICI Bank and Standard Chartered Bank (authorized dealers). By letters dated 07.12.96 and 18.01.97 Exchange Control Copies of bills of entry (in short, ECC - bills of entry) in relation to those imports were forwarded by the Company to the above mentioned Banks. As per the provisions of Exchange Control Manual (in short ECM), the authorized dealers had to submit the ECC-bills of entry submitted by the importers (the Company) to the Reserve Bank of India (in short RBI). The Company was under the bonafide impression that the documents submitted by it were forwarded by the authorized dealers to the RBI and that the RBI in turn had given due intimation to the Enforcement Directorate. The Company on 22.04.2004 received a telephonic communication from the office of the 3rd Respondent viz., Directorate of Enforcement, stating that it had passed various orders on 27.01.04 imposing a total penalty of Rs. 9,33,63,453/- on the Company on the ground that it had contravened the provisions of Sections 8(3) , 8(4) of FERA read with Sub-sections (3) and (4) of Section 49 of FEMA. Copies of the orders dated 27.01.04 were then received by the Company on 22.04.04 on request. From those orders the Company came to know that the Directorate of Enforcement had issued four show cause notices dated 14.05.02 stating that the Company had contravened Section 8(3) , Section 8(4) of FERA read with para 7A.20 (Chapter 7) of ECM and was required to show cause why adjudication proceedings be not initiated against the Company under Section 49 of FEMA for contravention of the above mentioned provisions. Further, it was also stated that the Company had failed to furnish the required bills/information/documents and did not avail of the opportunity of hearing in spite of notices issued to them on 29.08.02, 27.10.03 and 01.12.03. Orders dated 27.01.04 also indicated that an appeal would lie before the Appellate Tribunal after depositing the amount of penalty imposed within 45 days from the date on which the order was served. Reference was also made to Section 19 read with Section 49(5)(a) of FEMA.

Held,

We have already indicated that Clause (b) of Sub-section (5) of Section 49 refers to appeal preferred and pending before the Appellate Board under FERA at the time of repeal. The said clause does not specifically refer to appeals preferred against adjudication orders passed under FEMA with reference to causes of action which arose under FERA. We have already noticed the right of appeal under FEMA has already been saved in respect of cause of action which arose under FERA however subject to the proviso to Sub-section (2) of Section 19 , in the case of belated appeals.

Above discussion will clearly demonstrate that Section 49 of FEMA does not seek to withdraw or take away the vested right of appeal in cases where proceedings were initiated prior to repeal of FERA on 01.06.2000 or after. On a combined reading of Section 49 of FEMA and Section 6 of General Clauses Act, it is clear that the procedure prescribed by FEMA only would be applicable in respect of an appeal filed under FEMA though cause of action arose under FERA. In fact, the time limit prescribed under FERA was taken away under the *proviso* to Sub-section (2) of Section 19 and the Tribunal has been conferred with wide powers to condone delay if the appeal is not filed within forty-five days prescribed, provided sufficient cause is shown. Therefore, the findings rendered by the Tribunal as well as the High Court that the Tribunal does not have jurisdiction to condone the delay beyond the date prescribed under FERA is not a correct understanding of the law on the subject.We, therefore, hold that the Appellate Tribunal can entertain the appeal after the prescribed period of 45 days if it is satisfied, that there was sufficient cause for not filing the appeal within the said period. We are therefore inclined to set aside the orders passed by the Tribunal and the High Court and remit the matter back to the Tribunal for fresh consideration in accordance with law on the basis of the findings recorded by us. We order accordingly.

The appeals stand disposed of accordingly.

FIVE

IDBI Trusteeship Services Ltd. Vs. Hubtown Ltd., 2016

Hon'ble Judges/Coram: Kurian Joseph and Rohinton Fali Nariman, JJ.

Acts/Rules/Orders:

Code of Civil Procedure, 1908 (CPC) - Section 115; Order 14, Order 37 Rule 2, Order 37 Rule 3, Order 37 Rule 3(2), Order 37 Rule 3(3), Order 37 Rule 3(4), Order 37 Rule 3(5), Order 37 Rule 3(6); Foreign Exchange Management Act, 1999 - Regulation 4, Regulation 5;Constitution of India - Article 136

Equivalent Citation: 2017(1)ABR469, 2017(170)AIC77, AIR2016SC5321, 2017(2)AJR484, 2017(1)ALD76, 2017 (120) ALR 715, 2017(1)ALT47, II(2017)BC280(SC), 2016 (4) CCC 221 , 123(2017)CLT139, (2017)3CompLJ327(SC), 2016(6)CTC647, 2017(I)CLR(SC)12, 2017-2-LW193, 2017(2)MhLj770, (2016)8MLJ390, 2017 135 RD60, 2016(12)SCALE24, (2017)1SCC568, [2017]140SCL189(SC), MANU/SC/1490/2016

No. of pages in the Original Judgement: 15

Case Note:

Civil - Leave to defend suit - Present appeal - Arises out of Summons for a judgment - Petitioner a debenture trustee filed summary suit - Original Side of the Bombay High Court - Enforce the rights arising out of Corporate Guarantee - Executed by Respondent-defendant - In 2009 and 2010, Nederlandse Financierings-Maatschappij voor Ontwikkelingslanden N.V. (FMO) - Invested in certain equity shares and compulsorily convertible debentures (CCDs) of Vinca - Result of said investment - FMO currently holds 10% of equity shares of Vinca - 3 CCDs in Vinca - Further, Defendant owns 49% equity of Vinca - Entitled to 49% voting rights and economic interest in Vinca - Remaining 41% of voting rights - Owned by individual promoters - Said monies invested by FMO - Used by Vinca to subscribe to certain Optionally Partially Convertible Debentures (OPCDs) - Plaintiff-India's largest Trusteeship Company - Provides wide spectrum of Trusteeship Services - Plaintiff appointed as Debenture Trustee - Vide Debenture Trust Deeds - Relation to Vinca's investment in OPCDs issued by Amazia and Rubix - As per Debenture Trust Deeds, Vinca subscribed to certain OPCDs - Carrying viable running coupon and a back ended coupon - Ensure an internal rate of return - Plaintiff states - Proceeds obtained by Amazia and Rubix - Issue of OPCSs to Vinca to be applied - Projects compliant with Indian Foreign Direct Investment law - Applicable to townships, housing, built-up infrastructure and construction development projects - To secure said OPCDs and to ensure due and punctual payment - Under Debenture Guarantee Deeds - Vide Corporate Guarantee Deed - Issued an unconditional, absolute and irrevocable guarantee - Favour of Plaintiff - Defaults committed by Amazia and Rubix - Hence, plaintiff constrained to issue notices - Clause 33.1 of Debenture Trust Deeds - No response forthcoming from Amazia and/or Rubix - Consequently, Plaintiff exercised its right of early redemption - Issued redemption notices - Called upon both to fully redeem all the OPCDs - Despite repeated reminders, both failed - Neglected to pay the amount due - Payable in terms of Debenture Trust Deeds - Consequently, Plaintiff constrained to issue Demand certificate - Enforcement of Guarantee - No reply received to said Demand Certificate - Ld. Single Judge rejected Plaintiff's submission - Vide impugned judgment - Whether the judgment in Mechelec's case continues to be law even after the amendment of Order XXXVII in 1976 - Whether the Defendant be provided with a leave to defend the suit

Brief facts of the case:

The present appeal arises out of a Summons for a judgment in a Summary Suit filed on the original side of the Bombay High Court, by the Appellant-Plaintiff, a debenture trustee, to enforce rights that arise out of a Corporate Guarantee executed by the Respondent-defendant.

In 2009 and 2010, Nederlandse Financierings-Maatschappij voor Ontwikkelingslanden N.V. (FMO) invested in certain equity shares and compulsorily convertible debentures (CCDs) of Vinca Developer Private Limited (Vinca). As a result of the said investment, FMO currently holds (i) 10% of the equity of Vinca through Class A shares and is entitled to 10%

of the voting rights and economic interest in Vinca by virtue thereof; and (ii) 3 CCDs in Vinca. Further, as on date, the Defendant owns 49% of the equity of Vinca through Class A shares and is entitled to 49% of the voting rights and economic interest in Vinca by virtue thereof. The remaining 41% Class A equity shares in Vinca are owned by the individual promoters of the Defendant. The said monies invested by FMO into Vinca were then used by Vinca to subscribe to certain optionally partially convertible debentures (OPCDs).

Held,

Coming to the facts of the present case:

a. It is clear that a sum of ` 418 crores has been paid by FMO, the Dutch company, to Vinca for purchase of shares as well as compulsorily convertible debentures. This transaction by itself is not alleged to be violative of the FEMA Regulations.

b. The suit is filed only on invocation of the Corporate Guarantee which on its terms is unconditional. It may be added that it is not the Defendant's case that the said Corporate Guarantee is wrongly invoked.

c. Payment under the said Guarantee is to the debenture trustee, an Indian company, for and on behalf of Vinca, another Indian company, so that *prima facie* again there is no infraction of the FEMA Regulations.

d. Since FMO becomes a 99% holder of Vinca after the requisite time period has elapsed, FMO may at that stage utilise the funds received pursuant to the overall structure agreements in India. If this is so, again *prima facie* there is no breach of FEMA Regulations.

e. At the stage that FMO wishes to repatriate such funds, RBI permission would be necessary. If RBI permission is not granted, then again there would be no infraction of FEMA Regulations.

f. The judgment in Immami Appa Rao's case would be attracted only if the illegal purpose is fully carried out, and not otherwise.

Based on the aforesaid, it cannot be said that the Defendant has raised a substantial defence to the claim made in the suit. Arguably at the highest, as held by the learned Single Judge, even if a triable issue may be said to arise on the application of the FEMA Regulations, nevertheless, we are left with a real doubt about the Defendant's good faith and the genuineness of such a triable issue. ` 418 crores has been stated to be utilized and submerged in a building construction project, with payments under the structured arrangement mentioned above admittedly being made by the concerned parties until 2011, after which payments stopped being made by them. The defence thus raised appears to us to be in the realm of being 'plausible but improbable'. This being the case, the Plaintiff needs to be protected. In our opinion, the Defendant will be granted leave to defend the suit only if it deposits in the Bombay High Court the principal sum of ` 418 crores invested by FMO, or gives security for the said amount of ` 418 crores, to the satisfaction of the Prothonotary and Senior Master, Bombay High Court within a period of three months from today. The appeal is accordingly allowed, and the judgment of the Bombay High Court is set aside.

We further direct that the suit be tried expeditiously, preferably within a period of one year from the date of this judgment, uninfluenced by any observations made by us herein.

SIX

DROPTI DEVI AND ORS. VS. UNION OF INDIA (UOI) AND ORS., 2012

Hon'ble Judges/Coram: R.M. Lodha and H.L. Gokhale, JJ.

Relevant Section:

Conservation of Foreign Exchange and Prevention of Smuggling Activities Act, 1974 - Section 3(1)

Equivalent Citation: 2012ACR2507, 2012(116)AIC40, AIR2012SC2550, 2012 (78) ACC 761, 2012(3)ALT(Cri)SC347, III(2012)CCR95(SC), 2012(4)CTC858, 2012(4)J.L.J.R.45, JT2012(6)SC159, 2012(3)RCR(Criminal)687, 2012(6)SCALE80, (2012)7SCC499, MANU/SC/0506/2012

No. of pages in the Original Judgement: 14

Case Note:

Constitution - Validity of Provision - Section 3(1) of Conservation of Foreign Exchange and Prevention of Smuggling Activities Act, 1974 (COFEPOSA); Foreign Exchange Management Act, 1999 (FEMA); Section 56 of Foreign Exchange Regulation Act, 1973 (FERA) - Held, Constitution recognized preventive detention though, it took away liberty of a person without any enquiry or trial - Preventive detention resulted in negation of personal liberty of an individual - It deprived an individual freedom and was not seen as compatible with rule of law - Yet framers of Constitution placed same in Part III of Constitution - Constitution perceived preventive detention as a potential solution to prevent danger to state security - Security of State being legitimate goal, this Court had upheld power of Parliament and State Legislatures to enact laws of preventive detention -

With specific reference to COFEPOSA, a nine-Judge Bench of this Court in case of Attorney General for India and Ors. v. Amratlal Prajivandas and Ors. had held that enactment was relatable to Entry 3 of List III inasmuch as it provided for preventive detention for reasons connected with security of State as well as maintenance of supplies and services essential to community besides Entry 9 of List I - Where validity of any Ninth Schedule law had been upheld by this Court, it would not be open to challenge such law again on principles declared by judgment - COFEPOSA was specified in Ninth Schedule at Item No. 104 - Constitutional validity of COFEPOSA had already been upheld by this Court in case of Amratlal Prajivandas and, therefore, it was not open for challenge again - Provisions of FERA and FEMA differed in some respects - FEMA did not have provision for prosecution and punishment like Section 56 of FERA and its enforcement for default was through civil imprisonment - Insofar as conservation and/ or augmentation of foreign exchange was concerned, restrictions in FEMA continued to be as rigorous as they were in FERA - FEMA continued with regime of rigorous control of foreign exchange and dealing in foreign exchange was permitted only through authorised person - Conservation and augmentation of foreign exchange continued to be as important as it was under FERA - Restrictions on dealings in foreign exchange continued to be as rigorous in FEMA as they were in FERA and control of Government over foreign exchange continued to be as complete and full as it was in FERA - Whole intent and idea behind COFEPOSA was to prevent violation of foreign exchange Regulations or smuggling activities which had serious and deleterious effect on national economy - Relevance of provision for preventative detention of anti-social elements indulging in smuggling and violation and manipulation of foreign exchange in COFEPOSA continued even after repeal of FERA - There was no constitutional mandate that, preventive detention could not exist for an act where such act was not a criminal offence and did not provide for punishment - An act might not be declared as an offence under law but, still for such an act, which was an illegal activity, law could provide for preventive detention if such act was prejudicial to state security - Essential concept of preventive detention was not to punish a person for what he had done but to prevent him from doing an illegal activity prejudicial to security of State - Law of preventative detention armed State with precautionary action and must be seen as such of course, safeguards that Constitution and preventive detention laws provide must be strictly insisted upon whenever Court was called upon to examine legality and validity of an order of preventive detention - There was no merit in challenge to constitutional validity of impugned part of Section 3(1) of COFEPOSA - Petition rejectedConstitution - Leave to make Additional Prayer - Application filed for permitting Petitioners to make an additional prayer that "this Court might be pleased to quash detention order" - Held, in view of order dated July 13, 2010 passed by this Court, Petitioners could not be permitted to challenge order of detention until its execution - Leave to make additional prayer for quashing detention order dated September 23, 2009 by means of Application did not deserve to be granted - Application rejected

Held,

In view of the above, the leave to make additional prayer for quashing the detention order dated September 23, 2009 by means of criminal miscellaneous application does not deserve to be granted and is rejected. However, it is clarified that after the execution of the detention order, the Petitioners shall be at liberty to challenge the detention order in accordance with law.

Since we have rejected the criminal miscellaneous application, the argument of the Learned Counsel for the Petitioners that the impugned order of detention was passed way back on September 23, 2009; the impugned order was preventive in nature and the maximum period of detention as per law is one year, which would have lapsed by now and, therefore, no purpose for the execution of the detention order survives is noted to be rejected. The detention order could not be executed because of the contumacious conduct of the second Petitioner and, therefore, he cannot take advantage of his own wrong.

Writ petition and criminal miscellaneous application, for the reasons indicated above, are liable to be rejected and are rejected.

PPP

SEVEN

Raj Kumar Shivhare Vs. Assistant Director, Directorate of Enforcement and Ors., 2010

Hon'ble Judges/Coram: G.S. Singhvi and A.K. Ganguly, JJ.

Relevant Section:

Foreign Exchange Management Act, 1999 - Section 30; Family Courts Act, 1984 - Section 19; Code of Civil Procedure, 1908 (CPC) - Section 104

Equivalent Citation: 2010(90)AIC169, AIR2010SC2239, [2010]98CLA82(SC), 2010(253)ELT3(S.C.), JT2010(4)SC54, (2010)4MLJ964(SC), 2010(3)RCR(Civil)483, (2010)4SCC772, [2010]SCR608, MANU/SC/0249/2010

No. of pages in the Original Judgement: 6

Case Note:

FEMA - Jurisdiction - Section 35 of FEMA, Article 136 of Constitution of India and Section 14 of Limitation Act, 1963 - Whether Petition filed is maintainable subject to limitations? - Held, liability of Appellant is not created under any common law principle but, it is clearly a statutory liability and for which statutory remedy is an appeal under liability of the Appellant is not created under any common law principle but, it is clearly a statutory liability and for which the statutory remedy is an appeal under Section 35 of FEMA, subject to the limitations contained therein - A writ petition in facts of case is therefore clearly not maintainable subject to limitations contained therein - A writ petition in facts of case is therefore clearly not maintainable - Writ petition is not ordinarily maintainable to challenge an order of Tribunal - In view of Court's jurisdiction under Article 136 of Constitution - Court give liberty to Appellant to file an appeal before an appropriate High Court within meaning of Explanation to Section 35 of FEMA and if such an appeal is filed within a period of thirty days appellate forum will consider question of limitation and having regard to provision of Section 14 of Act ,1963 and also having regard to fact that Appellant was bona-fide in pursuing his case under Article 226 of Constitution before Delhi High Court and then appealed before this Court - Appeal dismissed

Brief facts of the case:

The appellant, along with another person, were issued a notice dated 12.1.2005 under Section 3(c) of the Foreign Exchange Management Act, 1999 (FEMA) for receiving unauthorized payments worth Rs. 5 crores under instructions from persons living outside India in connection with his illegal cricket betting operation. He was also asked to explain why the amount of Rs. 1 lac, confiscated during search from his residence, should not be credited to the account of the Central Government under Section 13(2) of FEMA, 1999.As the charges were proved against him, a penalty of Rs. 2 crores was imposed on him and the confiscated money was disposed of according to Section 13(2) vide order dated 29.02.2008.

On appeal to the Appellate Tribunal under Section 19(2) of the Act, the Tribunal passed the order dated 17.7.2008, the concluding portion whereof is quoted above

Held,

The decision in **Ambica Industries** (supra) is also on the question of part of cause of action under Article 226(2) of the Constitution of India. For the aforesaid reasons, the decision in **Ambica Industries** (supra) is not of much relevance in the facts of the case in hand.

For the reasons discussed above, this Court is of the opinion a writ petition is not ordinarily maintainable to challenge an order of the Tribunal. We, therefore, dismiss the appeal, of course for reasons which are different from the ones given by the High Court in dismissing the writ petition.

In view of this Court's jurisdiction under Article 136 of the Constitution, we give liberty to the appellant, if so advised, to file an appeal before an appropriate High Court within the meaning of Explanation to Section 35 of FEMA and if such an appeal is filed within a period of thirty days from today, the appellate forum will consider the question of limitation sympathetically having regard to the provision of Section 14 of the Limitation Act and also having regard to the fact that the appellant was bona-fide pursuing his case under Article 226 of the Constitution before the Delhi High Court and then its appeal before this Court.

With the aforesaid direction, the appeal is dismissed. The parties are left to bear their own costs.

EIGHT

S.K. SINHA VS. VIDEOCON INTERNATIONAL LTD. AND ORS., 2008

Hon'ble Judges/Coram: C.K. Thakker and P.P. Naolekar, JJ.

Relevant Section:

Foreign Exchange Management Act, 1999 - Section 49; Foreign Exchange Regulation Act, 1973 [Repealed] - Section 18; Code of Criminal Procedure, 1973 (CrPC) - Section 200; Indian Penal Code, 1860 (IPC) - Section 161

Equivalent Citation: 2008(64)AIC150, AIR2008SC1213, 2008(2)ALD(Cri)94, 2008 (61) ACC 371, 2008(2)ALT(Cri)279, I(2008)CCR256(SC), [2009]148CompCas261(SC), 2008CriLJ1636, 2008GLH(1)479, [2008(3)JCR56(SC)], JT2008(2)SC8, (2008)39OCR704, 2008(2)RCR(Criminal)38, RLW2008(3)SC2147, 2008(2)SCALE23, (2008)2SCC492, [2008]81SCL507(SC), MANU/SC/7011/2008

No. of pages in the Original Judgement: 8

Case Note:

Criminal - Issuance of process vis--vis cognizance by Criminal Court - Limitation - Sections 202, 204 of the Code of Criminal Procedure, 1973 - Section 49(3), FEMA - Appellant-complainant filed Criminal Complaint against the Company alleging that the Company had received an amount of Rs. 44,04,00,000 but it failed to take steps to realize export proceeds amounting to Rs. 16,60,00,000 within the stipulated period of six months thereby contravening Section 18(2), 18(3) r/w Section 68(1), punishable under Section 56(1)(ii) of FERA - On May 24, 2002, the Chief Metropolitan Magistrate took cognizance of the offence and issued summons to the accused - On February 3, 2003, the Chief Metropolitan Magistrate issued process requiring the respondents to appear before the Court and answer the charge under FERA -Respondents filed a petition being Criminal Writ Petition in the High Court seeking quashing of criminal proceedings on the ground that cognizance was taken by the Court after the period of limitation - High Court quashed the proceedings initiated against the respondents on the ground that cognizance could be said to have been taken when process was issued and since process was issued in February, 2003, the proceedings were time-barred - Whether issuance of process in a criminal case is one and the same thing or can be equated with taking cognizance by a Criminal Court and if the period of initiation of criminal proceedings has elapsed at the time of issue of process by a Court, the proceedings should be quashed as barred by limitation - Held, cognizance of the offence was taken by the Chief Metropolitan Magistrate on the same day on which the complaint was filed - Under Section 202, what a Magistrate is called upon to see is whether there is sufficient ground for proceeding with the matter and not whether there is sufficient ground for conviction of the accused - 'Initiation of Proceedings', different from 'commencement of proceedings' covered by Chapter XVI - Initiation of proceedings must precede commencement of proceedings - Without initiation of proceedings under Chapter XIV, there cannot be commencement of proceedings before a Magistrate under Chapter XVI - Order of issuance of process on February 3, 2003 by the Court was in pursuance of and consequent to taking cognizance of an offence on May 24, 2002 - Cognizance well within the period prescribed by Section 49(3), FEMA - High Court was not right in equating taking cognizance with issuance of process and in holding that the complaint was barred by law and criminal proceedings were liable to be quashed - Appeal allowed

Ratio Decidendi:

If Order of issuance of process by the Court was taken in pursuance of and consequent to taking cognizance of an offence such cognizance has to be held well within the period prescribed by Section 49(3), FEMA.

Brief facts of the case:

To appreciate the controversy raised in the appeal instituted by the Chief Enforcement Officer, Enforcement Directorate, Government of India (appellant herein), few relevant facts may be noted.

Respondent No. 1-M/s. Videocon International Ltd. ('Company' for short) is a 'Public Limited Company' incorporated under the Companies Act, 1956 having its business at Mumbai and Aurangabad in the State of Maharashtra. On October 13, 1989, the Company entered into an agreement with Radio Export (Moscow) for the supply of colour tubes, electrolytic capacitors, transformers, etc., for Rs. 44,04,00,000/-. The payment was made by respondent No. 1 Company to Japanese and Korean suppliers. But before any payment could be received by respondent No. 1 from the USSR Company, there was political turmoil in the USSR and payment to foreign suppliers was disrupted. On January 5, 1993, Additional Director General, Directorate of Revenue Intelligence, Mumbai addressed a letter to the appellant alerting him about the activities of the Company in connection with the agreement to supply television sets to Radio Export, Moscow. Based on the information forwarded by the Directorate of Revenue Intelligence, Bombay, the appellant addressed two letters to the Chief Manager of Indian Bank, Nariman Point, Bombay requesting the Bank to supply details of the export outstanding of the Company. Indian Bank supplied necessary information and indicated that the export outstanding of the Company was Rs. 16,60,00,000/-. The Reserve Bank of India turned down the request of the Company for reimbursement of differential amount remaining unpaid on the ground that the exports were effected from Korea and Japan and not from India and the Company was not entitled to reimbursement. In pursuance of the summons issued under Section 40 of the Foreign Exchange Regulation Act, 1973 (hereinafter referred to as 'FERA'), Raj Kumar Dhoot, Director of the Company appeared before the Department on April 25, 1999 and made a statement that there was an agreement between the Company and M/s Radio Export, Moscow for supply of two lakh television sets and other equipments for Rs. 44,04,00,000/-. The amount was received by the Company through State Bank of India, Overseas Branch, Bombay. He further stated that the television sets had been procured from Korea and Japan who had been paid equivalent to Rs. 19,00,00,000/- in foreign exchange. Export bills raised from the sale to M/s Radio Export, Moscow were equivalent to Rs. 16,00,00,000/-. Whereas the contract with the suppliers in Korea and Japan stipulated payment in US Dollars, the contract with the USSR Company required payment in Indian Rupees. Since the value of Rupee against the US Dollar fell down, the Company had to pay more Rupees to their foreign suppliers. On June 1, 2000, FERA was replaced by the Foreign Exchange Management Act, 1999 (hereinafter referred to as 'FEMA').

Held,

In our opinion, it would not be necessary for us to express any opinion one way or the other on the larger question. We have already held in the earlier part of the judgment that in the case on hand, cognizance of an offence had already been taken by the Chief Metropolitan Magistrate, Mumbai on May 24, 2002, well within the period prescribed by Sub-section (3) of Section 49 of FEMA within two years of coming into force of the Act from June 1, 2000. We, therefore, express no opinion on the question raised by the learned Counsel for the respondent.

As regards quashing of proceedings on merits, the learned Counsel for the appellant is right in submitting that the High Court has not at all touched the merits of the case and proceedings were not quashed on the ground that the provisions of FERA do not apply to the case before the Court. The High Court dealt with only one point as to whether the proceedings were liable to be quashed on the ground that they were time-barred and upholding the contention of the accused, passed the impugned order. As we are of the view that the High Court was not right in quashing the proceedings on the ground of limitation, the order deserves to be set aside by remitting the matter to the Chief Metropolitan Magistrate, Mumbai to be decided in accordance with law. We may, however, clarify that it is open to the respondents to take all contentions including the contention as to applicability or otherwise of FERA to the facts of the case. As and when such question will be raised, the Court will pass an appropriate order in accordance with law.For the foregoing reasons, the appeal is allowed. The order passed by the High Court is set aside and it is held that cognizance of the offence had already been taken by the competent Criminal Court i.e. Chief Metropolitan Magistrate, Mumbai on May 24, 2002 and it could not be said that the proceedings were barred by Section 49(3) of FEMA. The Chief Metropolitan Magistrate will now proceed to consider the matter in accordance with law. All contentions of all parties are kept open except the one decided by us in this appeal. Since the matter is very old, the Court will give priority and will decide it as expeditiously as possible, preferably before June 30, 2008. Ordered accordingly.

NINE

Kanwar Natwar Singh Vs. Director of Enforcement and Ors., 2010

Hon'ble Judges/Coram: B. Sudershan Reddy and S.S. Nijjar, JJ.

Relevant Section:

Foreign Exchange Management Act, 1999 - Section 4; Section 13; Indian Penal Code, 1860 (IPC) - Section 193; Section 228

Equivalent Citation: [2010]99CLA415(SC), [2010]160CompCas301(SC), [2011]330ITR374(SC), JT2010(11)SC282, 2010(4)RCR(Criminal)813, 2010(10)SCALE401, (2010)13SCC255, MANU/SC/0795/2010

No. of pages in the Original Judgement: 9

Case Note:

FEMA - Notice - Rule 4(1) of Foreign Exchange Management (Adjudication Proceedings and Appeal) Rules, 2000 - Adjudicating Authority's refusal to supply all documents as demanded by Appellants led to filing of writ petitions by Appellants in High Court which was dismissed - Hence, this Appeal - Whether, a notice served with show cause notice under Rule 4(1) was entitled to demand to furnish all documents in possession of Adjudicating Authority - Held, Appellants insisted for supply of all documents in possession of Authority and such demand was based on vague, indefinite and irrelevant grounds - Appellants were not sure as to whether, they were asking for copies of documents in possession of

Adjudicating Authority or in possession of authorized officer who lodged complaint - The only object in making such demand was to obstruct proceedings and Appellants, was able to achieve their object as was evident from fact that inquiry initiated as early as in year 2006 still did not even commence - Adjudicating Authority could not deal with complaint expeditiously which was required to be disposed of within one year from date of receipt of complaint - Hence, Appellants were entitled to all defence that may be available to them in law - Appeal dismissed.

Ratio Decidendi:

Due process of law cannot be misused."

Brief facts of the case:

A complaint in writing has been filed by an officer authorized against the appellants under Sub-section (3) of Section 16 of the Foreign Exchange Management Act, 1999 (hereinafter referred to as 'FEMA' or 'the Act') in which certain serious allegations have been levelled against the appellants which we are not required to notice in detail. The gravamen of the complaint is that the appellants along with others, jointly and severally, without general or special permission of the Reserve Bank of India dealt in and acquired Foreign Exchange totaling US $ 8,98,027.79 in respect of two oil contracts with SOMO of Iraq. Out of the said amount, the appellants and others jointly and severally, without the required permission of the Reserve Bank of India made payment and transferred Foreign Exchange of US $ 7,48,550 to the credit of specified account with Jordan National Bank, Jordan i.e., to persons resident outside India, in fulfillment of precondition imposed by SOMO for allocation of oil under aforesaid two contracts, in contravention of the provisions of FEMA. It is further alleged that the appellants and others, jointly and severally, without the required permission of the Reserve Bank of India transferred Foreign Exchange of US $ 1,46,247.23 being the commission amount in respect of two oil contracts with SOMO to the account with the Barclays Bank, London in contravention of the provisions of the Act. The appellants together with others jointly and severally failed to take all reasonable steps to repatriate the aforesaid Foreign Exchange within the stipulated period and in the prescribed manner, in contravention of the provisions of FEMA read with Regulations, 2000. In addition to the above, some other allegations also levelled against appellant No. 2. The Adjudicating Authority having received the said complaint, set the law in motion and accordingly issued a notice to the appellants under the provisions of FEMA read with the Rules, requiring them to show cause why an inquiry should not be held against them.

3. The appellants having received the show cause notice, instead of submitting their reply, required the Adjudicating Authority to furnish "copies of all the documents in...possession in respect of the instant case, including the 83000 documents allegedly procured by one Virender Dayal from USA in connection with the instant case...." This seemingly innocuous request ultimately turned out to be the origin of this avoidable litigation. The fact remains that the copies of all such documents as relied upon by the Adjudicating Authority were furnished. The Authority, however, declined to furnish copies of other documents and decided to hold an inquiry in accordance with the provisions of FEMA and the Rules.

Held,

The appellants insisted for supply of all documents in possession of the Authority and such demand is based on vague, indefinite and irrelevant grounds. The appellants are not sure as to whether they are asking for the copies of the documents in possession of the Adjudicating Authority or in possession of authorized officer who lodged the complaint. The only object in making such demand is obviously to obstruct the proceedings and the appellants, to some extent, have been able to achieve their object as is evident from the fact that the inquiry initiated as early as in the year 2006 still did not even commence.

We are constrained to take note of the fact that it is on account of continuous unreasonable requests on the part of the appellants, the Adjudicating Authority could not deal with the complaint expeditiously which is required to be disposed of within one year from the date of receipt of the complaint. We accordingly direct the Adjudicating Authority to deal with the complaint as expeditiously as possible and every endeavor shall be made to dispose of the complaint finally at the earliest. No unreasonable request for adjournment shall be entertained by the Adjudicating Authority.

However, we make it clear that the Authority shall make inquiry into the allegations made in the complaint strictly in accordance with the law and uninfluenced by the observations if any made in this order. We have not expressed any opinion whatsoever on the merits of the case. The appellants are entitled to all the defence that may be available to them in law.

For all the aforesaid reasons, the appeals are dismissed with costs

TEN

Kamlesh Kumar and Ors. Vs. The State of Jharkhand and Ors., 2013

Hon'ble Judges/Coram: H.L. Gokhale and Madan B. Lokur, JJ.

Acts/Rules/Orders:

Code of Criminal Procedure, 1973 (CrPC) - Section 406; Section 407; Section 407(1)(c); Section 431; Section 435; Section 439; Constitution Of India - Article 14, Article 142, Article 19, Article 227, Article 235; Foreign Exchange Management Act, 1999 - Section 49(4); Section 13, Section 18, Section 18A, Section 19, Section 44, Section 45, Section 56, Section 56(1), Section 57, Section 58, Section 61, Section 61(1), Foreign Exchange Regulation Act, 1973 [repealed] - Section 62, Section 64(2), Section 9(1)(a); Negotiable Instruments Act, 1881 - Section 138

Equivalent Citation: 2013X AD (S.C.) 491, 2013(132)AIC182, 2013(4)AJR589, 2014 (84) ACC 317, 2014 (1) ALT (Crl.) 273 (A.P.), 2013(4)BLJ138, I(2014)CCR134(SC), 2014CriLJ22, 2014(1)J.L.J.R.411, 2013(4)JCC2752, JT2013(13)SC155, 2014(1)PLJR497, 2013(4)RCR(Criminal)754, 2013(12)SCALE216, (2013)15SCC460, 2014 (1) SCJ 297, MANU/SC/0986/2013

No. of pages in the Original Judgement: 9

Case Note:

Jurisdiction - Transfer of cases - Sections 56, 61, 62 of Foreign Exchange Regulation Act, 1973 (FERA) - High Court passed a resolution to empower

Special Judge, CBI to try cases of FEMA, accordingly a notification was issued by State of Jharkhand on empowering Special Judge CBI (AHD Scam cases) to try cases under FEMA and pursuant to that notification Complaint filed before Chief Judicial Magistrate was transferred for trial to Court of Additional Judicial Commissioner cum Special Judge - However Single Judge of High Court dismissed Writ Petitions filed by Petitioner for quashing of said notification - Hence, this Special Leave Petitions - Whether, State Government had jurisdiction to authorise Special Judge to try these cases under FERA - Held, Petitioners were being prosecuted under Section 56 of FERA, wherein maximum punishment that could be awarded was up to seven years - Such offences were triable by Magistrate of first Class provided those offences were cognizable offences - It was merely lawful for Magistrate to try offences under Section 61 of FERA Act , but Court of Magistrate was not a Court of exclusive jurisdiction - Offence was a non-cognizable one and therefore it was not mandatory that it ought to have been tried only by Magistrate of First Class - Thus Petitioner could not claim that Magistrate had special jurisdiction to try offence and that State could not transfer case to Sessions Judge - It could not be said that Magistrate's Court had an exclusive jurisdiction to try cases relating to violations of provisions of FERA and those cases could not be transferred to Special Judge - In case Accused were common many of witnesses would be common and so also their evidence - However Section 407 (1) (c) of Cr.P.C. laid down that, where it would tend to general convenience of parties or witnesses or where it was expedient for ends of justice, High Court could transfer such a case for trial to a Court of Sessions - That did not mean that High Court could not transfer cases by exercising its administrative power of superintendence which was available to it under Article 227 of Constitution of India – Special Leave Petitions dismissed.

Ratio Decidendi:

"Court either in administration side or in judicial side has absolute jurisdiction to transfer any criminal cases pending before one competent Court to be heard and decided by another Court within jurisdiction of Court."

Brief facts of case:

The above referred Dr. K.M. Prasad, father of the Petitioners, was working earlier as the Director of Animal Husbandry department, Government of Bihar. He is being prosecuted along with some others by the Central Bureau of Investigation (C.B.I.) in the Court of Special Judge at Ranchi for conspiracy to defraud the State Government to the extent of Rs. 7,09,92,000/- during 1980-90 on the basis of fake allotment letters purportedly issued by him for the purchase of medicines. It is claimed that fake supplies were shown as made by the suppliers, and the money withdrawn towards such fake allotments was misappropriated by the accused persons.

During the course of investigation it was realized that the amount involved was much more, i.e. Rs. 19,81,66,460/- approximately, and that the accused Dr. K.M. Prasad had acquired huge movable as well as immovable assets in his own name, and in the name of his children and others at different places. The said Dr. K.M. Prasad and his children were also therefore prosecuted in the case arising out of this investigation, and charges have already been submitted by the CBI against them, and the cases are pending in the court of Special Judge CBI at Ranchi.

Held,

Reliance was placed by learned Counsel for the Petitioners on a Division Bench decision of the Delhi High Court in ***A.S. Impex Ltd. v. Delhi High Court***MANU/DE/1081/2003 : 107 (2003) DLT 734. This reliance is not only misplaced but, in my opinion, that decision should be overruled as not laying down the correct law.

51. In that case, the High Court administratively decided to transfer cases filed Under Section 138 of the Negotiable Instruments Act, 1881 on or before 31st December 2001 and pending before the Magistrates to the Additional Sessions Judges. A notification for transfer of cases was accordingly issued and this was struck down by the Delhi High Court by, inter alia, relying on the law laid down in ***Antulay***. As already noted above, the law laid down in ***Antulay*** has limited application and is not relevant to cases such as the one we are dealing with. This was clearly explained in ***Ranbir Yadav*** but the Delhi High Court ignored the observations of this Court without much ado by holding: "In that case the Court transferred the case from the Court of one Magistrate to the Court of another Magistrate for the reason that there was shortage of accommodation in the first Court. That is not the case in hand. It was not a case where the jurisdiction was transferred from the Court of Magistrate to the Court of Sessions." The Delhi High Court also proceeded on an erroneous basis that the exercise of plenary administrative power available to the High Court to transfer cases meant the bypassing or circumventing of statutory provisions empowering Magistrates to try cases Under Section 138 of the Negotiable Instruments Act, 1881 and conferring that jurisdiction on Additional Sessions Judges. The High Court did not

correctly appreciate the power available to a High Court under Article 227 of the Constitution.

The error in ***A.S. Impex*** was correctly understood by the Division Bench of the Delhi High Court in ***Mahender Singh v. High Court of Delhi***MANU/DE/0987/2008 : (2009) 151 Co. Cas 485 (Delhi) and in ***N.G. Sheth v. C.B.I.***MANU/DE/0979/2008 : 151 (2008) DLT 89. The Division Bench in both cases took a view different from that in ***A.S. Impex***. However, both decisions having been rendered by Division Benches, ***A.S. Impex***, could not be overruled. Therefore, I complete the formality and overrule ***A.S. Impex*** since it does not lay down the correct law in this regard.

For the reasons abovementioned, the Special Leave Petitions are dismissed.

PPP

ELEVEN

SHAILENDRA SWARUP VS. THE DEPUTY DIRECTOR, ENFORCEMENT DIRECTORATE, 2020

Hon'ble Judges/Coram: Ashok Bhushan and R. Subhash Reddy, JJ.

Acts/Rules/Orders:

Adjudication Proceedings & Appeal Rules, 1974 - Rule 3; Companies Act, 1956 - Section 291; Foreign Exchange Management Act, 1999 - Section 3, Section 4, Section 49; Foreign Exchange Regulation Act, 1973 - Section 8(3), Section 8(4), Section 50, Section 51, Section 68, Section 68(1); Negotiable Instruments Act, 1881 - Section 138, Section 141, Section 141(1), Section 141(2), Section 142

Equivalent Citation: AIR2020SC3890, 2020 (3) ALT (Crl.) 78 (A.P.), 2020(5)BLJ244, 2020(3)BomCR(Cri)88, [2020]159CLA12(SC), [2020]221CompCas758(SC), 2020(2)Crimes369(SC), 2020(373)ELT433(S.C.), 2021-1-LW(Crl)9, 2020(3)MLJ(Crl)721, 2020(3)RCR(Criminal)138, (2020)16SCC561, 2020 (6) SCJ 696, [2020]161SCL1(SC), MANU/SC/0544/2020

No. of pages in the Original Judgement: 11

Case Note:

FERA - Penalty - Deletion of - Sections 3,4,8(3), 8(4),49, 68 and 51 of Foreign Exchange Regulation Act, 1973 - Remittances were made by one company through its banker - Enforcement Directorate wrote to company for supplying invoices as well as purchase orders - Company provided for four transactions and Chartered Accountant's Certificates for balance amounts - Show cause notice was issued by Deputy Director, Enforcement Directorate to companny and its Directors, including Appellant - Show cause notice required to show cause in writing as to why adjudication proceedings as contemplated in Section 51 of Act should not be held for contravention - Company replied show cause notice - Directorate of Enforcement decided to hold proceedings as contemplated in Section 51 of Act read with Section 3 and 4 of Section 49 of Act - Deputy Director imposed penalty on Appellant for contravention of Section 8(3) read with 8(4) and Section 68 of Act - Aggrieved by order of imposing penalty on Appellant, appeal was filed by Appellant before Appellate Tribunal which was dismissed - Against order of Appellate Tribunal, appeal was filed in High Court which also dismissed - Hence, present appeal - Whether penalty on Appellant for contravention of Section 8(3) read with 8(4) and Section 68 of Act was sustainable.

Brief facts of the case:

The remittances were made by the one Company through its banker Standard Chartered Bank. The Reserve Bank of India issued a letter stating that despite reminder issued by the Authorised Dealer, company had not submitted the Exchange Control copy of the custom bills of Entry/Postal Wrappers as evidence of import of goods into India. Enforcement Directorate wrote to company for supplying invoices as well as purchase orders. Company provided for four transactions and Chartered Accountant's Certificates for balance amounts for which company's Bankers were unable to trace old records. A show cause notice was issued by the Deputy Director, Enforcement Directorate to company and its Directors, including the Appellant. The show cause notice required to show cause in writing as to why adjudication proceedings as contemplated in Section 51 of Foreign Exchange Regulation Act, 1973 should not be held for contravention. The Directorate of Enforcement decided to hold proceedings as contemplated in Section 51 of the FERA, 1973 read with Section 3 and 4 of Section 49 of FEMA. In the reply the Appellant stated that he is a practicing Advocate of the Supreme Court and was only a part-time, non-executive Director of company and he was never in the employment of the Company nor had executive role in the functions of the Company. It was further stated that the Appellant was never in charge of nor ever responsible for the conduct of business of the Company. Along with the reply an affidavit of the Company Secretary that the Appellant who was the Director of erstwhile

Company was only a part-time, Director of the said Company and never in charge of day to day business of the Company was also filed. The Deputy Director, Enforcement Directorate after hearing the Appellant, other Directors of the Company passed an order imposing a penalty on the Appellant for contravention of Section 8(3) read with 8(4) and Section 68 of FERA, 1973. Aggrieved by the order imposing penalty on the Appellant, appeal was filed by the Appellant before the Appellate Tribunal for Foreign Exchange which appeal came to be dismissed by the Appellate Tribunal. Against the order of the Appellate Tribunal, appeal was filed by the Appellant in High Court. The High Court by the impugned judgment had dismissed the appeal of the Appellant.

Held,

Learned Additional Solicitor General also submitted that all the three Courts have held and found contravention proved by the Appellant, this Court may not interfere with such conclusion. We have already noticed above that the plea of the Appellant that he was part-time, non-executive Director not in charge of the conduct of business of the Company at the relevant time was erroneously discarded by the authorities and the High Court and there is no finding by any of the authorities after considering the material that it was the Appellant who was responsible for the conduct of business of the Company at the relevant time. Thus, present is a case where the liability has been fastened on the Appellant without there being necessary basis for any such conclusion.

It is also relevant to notice that an order which was passed on 13.02.2004 by the Deputy Director in adjudication proceedings although with regard to different period, the plea of the Appellant that he was only a part-time, non-executive Director and not responsible of the conduct of business of the Company was accepted and notice was discharged against the Appellant. The order dated 13.02.2004 although related to different period but has categorically noticed the status of the Appellant as part-time non-executive Director. There being decision of Adjudicating Authority, in the recent past, passed on 13.02.2004, that the Appellant was only a part-time non-executive Director of MXL, there has to be some reasons for taking a contrary view by the adjudicating officer in order dated 31.03.2004 with regard to affairs of the same company, i.e., MXL.

In view of the foregoing discussions, we are of the view that the adjudicating officer has erroneously imposed penalty on the Appellant for the alleged offence Under Section 8(3), 8(4) and 68 of the FERA, 1973 which order was erroneously affirmed both by the Appellate Tribunal and the High Court.

In view of the aforesaid, this appeal deserves to be allowed, the judgments of the High Court as well as those of the adjudicating officer and the Appellate Tribunal are set aside. The appeal is allowed and the penalty imposed on the Appellant is set aside.

TWELVE

KETAN V. PAREKH VS. SPECIAL DIRECTOR, DIRECTORATE OF ENFORCEMENT AND ORS., 2011

Hon'ble Judges/Coram: G.S. Singhvi and S.J. Mukhopadhaya, JJ.

Relevant Section:

Foreign Exchange Management Act, 1999 - Section 3; Section 6(3); Arbitration and Conciliation Act, 1996 - Section 14; Central Excise Act, 1944 (Repealed) - Section 35

Equivalent Citation: 2012(110)AIC129, AIR2012SC683, [2012]108CLA1(SC), 2012(275)ELT3(S.C.), 2012-1-LW705, (2012)3MLJ141(SC), 2012(1)RCR(Civil)234, 2011(13)SCALE240, (2011)15SCC30, [2011]110SCL724(SC), 2012[28]S.T.R.195(S.C.), 2012(1)UJ143, MANU/SC/1421/2011

No. of pages in the Original Judgement: 11

Case Note:

FEMA - Exclusion of time of proceeding bonafide in court without jurisdiction- Section 14 of the Limitation Act - Whether Appellant were entitled to the benefit of Section 14 of the Limitation Act, 1963. Held, Section 14 of the Limitation Act cannot be relied upon for exclusion of the period during which the writ petitions filed by the Appellants remained pending before the Delhi High Court. There was not even a whisper in the applications filed by the Appellants that they had been prosecuting remedy before a wrong forum, i.e. the Delhi High Court with due diligence and in good faith. The prayer made in the applications was for condonation of delay and not for exclusion of the time spent in prosecuting the writ petitions before the Delhi High Court. Benefit of Section 14 of the Limitation Act could not be extended to the Appellants. All of them are well conversant with various statutory provisions. The very fact that they had engaged a group of eminent Advocates to present their cause before the Delhi and the Bombay High Courts shows that they had the assistance of legal experts and this seems to the reason why they invoked the jurisdiction of the Delhi High Court and not of the Bombay High Court despite the fact that they were residents of Bombay and have been contesting other matters including the proceedings pending before the Special Court at Bombay. It also appeared that the Appellants were sure that keeping in view their past conduct, the Bombay High Court may not interfere with the order of the Appellate Tribunal. Therefore, they took a chance before the Delhi High Court and succeeded in persuading learned Single Judge of the Court to entertain their prayer for stay of further proceedings before the Appellate Tribunal. The manner in which the Appellants prosecuted the writ petitions before the Delhi High Court leaves no room for doubt that they had done so with the sole object of delaying compliance of the direction given by the Appellate Tribunal and, by no stretch of imagination, it could be said that they were bona fide prosecuting remedy before a wrong forum. Rather, there was total absence of good faith, which is sine qua non for invoking Section 14 of the Limitation Act. Therefore, impugned Order upheld. Appeals dismissed.

Ratio Decidendi:

"Section 14 is not a provision for extension of period of limitation, but for exclusion of certain period while computing the period of limitation."

Brief facts of the case:

On an information received from the Reserve Bank of India that M/s. Classic Credit Ltd. and M/s. Panther Fincap and Management Services Ltd. had taken loan of 25 lakh shares each of DSQ Industries Ltd. on 1.3.2011 from M/s. Greenfield Investment Ltd, Mauritius and the Indus Ind Bank Ltd with whom M/s. Greenfield Investment Ltd. was maintaining NRE Account had informed that records did not indicate any such transaction, the Directorate of Enforcement, Mumbai conducted enquiries from different sources including Securities and Exchange Board of India, Shri Ketan Parekh, M/s. Integrated Enterprises (I) Ltd., Chennai and Indsec Securities and Finance

Ltd. Thereafter, show cause notice dated 23.9.2004 was issued to M/s. Greenfield Investments Ltd., Mauritius, Shri Pravin Guwalewala, Mauritius, Smt. Neena Guwalewala, Mauritius, Shri A.K. Sen, Mauritius, M/s. Classic Credit Ltd., Mumbai, M/s. Panther Fincap and Management Services Ltd., Mumbai, Shri Ketan Parekh, Shri Kartik K. Parekh, Shri Kirit Kumar N. Parekh and Shri Navin chandra Parekh for taking action against them for contravention of the provisions of the Act. After hearing the noticees, the Special Director of Enforcement, Mumbai (for short, `the Special Director') passed order dated 30.1.2006 and, whereby he held that some of the noticees had violated Sections 3(d) and 6(3)(e) of the Act and imposed penalty of Rs. 40 crores on M/s. Classic Credit Ltd.; Rs. 40 crores on M/s. Panther Fincap and Management Services Ltd.; Rs. 75 crores on M/s. Greenfield Investments Ltd.; Rs. 80 crores on Shri Ketan Parekh; Rs. 12 crores on Shri Kartik K. Parekh; Rs. 60 crores on Shri Pravin Guwalewala and Rs. 20 crores on Shri A.K. Sen with a direction that they shall deposit the amount within 45 days from the date of receipt of the order.

The Appellants challenged the aforesaid order by filing appeals under Section 19 of the Act. They also filed applications under Rule 10 of the Foreign Exchange Management (Adjudication Proceedings and Appeal) Rules, 2000 read with Section 19(1) of the Act for dispensing with the requirement of deposit of the amount of penalty. In paragraphs 4 to 8 of the application filed.

Held,

In this context, reference can usefully be made to the judgment of this Court in Benara Values Ltd. v. Commissioner of Central Excise MANU/SC/5093/2006 : (2006) 13 SCC 347. In that case, a two Judge Bench interpreted Section 35F of the Central Excise Act, 1944, which is pari materia to Section 19(1) of the Act, referred to the judgments in Siliguri Municipality v. Amalendu Das MANU/SC/0017/1984 : (1984) 2 SCC 436, Samarias Trading Company (P) Ltd. v. S. Samuel MANU/SC/0014/1984 : (1984) 4 SCC 666, Commissioner of Central Excise v. Dunlop India Ltd. MANU/SC/0169/1984 : (1985) 1 SCC 260 and observed:

Two significant expressions used in the provisions are "undue hardship to such person" and "safeguard the interests of the Revenue". Therefore, while dealing with the application twin requirements of considerations i.e. consideration of undue hardship aspect and imposition of conditions to safeguard the interests of the Revenue have to be kept in view.

As noted above there are two important expressions in Section 35F. One is undue hardship. This is a matter within the special knowledge of the applicant for waiver and has to be established by him. A mere assertion about undue hardship would not be sufficient. It was noted by this Court in S. Vasudeva v. State of Karnataka that under Indian conditions expression "undue hardship" is normally related to economic hardship. "Undue" which means something which is not merited by the conduct of the claimant, or is very much disproportionate to it. Undue hardship is caused when the hardship is not warranted by the circumstances.

For a hardship to be "undue" it must be shown that the particular burden to observe or perform the requirement is out of proportion to the nature of the requirement itself, and the benefit which the applicant would derive from compliance with it.

The word "undue" adds something more than just hardship. It means an excessive hardship or a hardship greater than the circumstances warrant.

The other aspect relates to imposition of condition to safeguard the interests of the Revenue. This is an aspect which the Tribunal has to bring into focus. It is for the Tribunal to impose such conditions as are deemed proper to safeguard the interests of the Revenue. Therefore, the Tribunal while dealing with the application has to consider materials to be placed by the assessee relating to undue hardship and also to stipulate conditions as required to safeguard the interests of the Revenue.

The same view was reiterated in Indu Nissan Oxo Chemicals Industries Ltd. v. Union of India MANU/SC/4581/2007 : (2007) 13 SCC 487 by considering proviso to Section 129-E of the Customs Act, 1962, which is almost identical to Section 19 of the Act.

In the result, the appeals are dismissed. Four weeks' further time is allowed to the Appellants to comply with the direction given by the Appellate Tribunal, failing which the appeals filed by them shall stand automatically dismissed. The parties are left to bear their own costs.

ÞÞÞ

THIRTEEN

UNION OF INDIA (UOI) AND ORS. VS. S. SRINIVASAN, 2012

Hon'ble Judges/Coram: B.S. Chauhan and Dipak Misra, JJ.

Acts/Rules/Orders:

Advocate Act, 1961 - Section 2 (a); Constitution Of India - Article 136, Article 14, Article 16, Article 233, Article 233(2), Article 234, Article 235, Article 236, Article 236(b); Foreign Exchange Management Act, 1999 - Section 15, Section 16, Section 17, Section 18, Section 19, Section 2(s), Section 20, Section 20(1), Section 21, Section 21(1), Section 21(1)(b), Section 21(2)(a), Section 22, Section 23, Section 25, Section 26, Section 27, Section 28, Section 39, Section 46, Section 46(2), Section 5; Section 52

Equivalent Citation: 2012(116)AIC150, 2012(281)ELT3(S.C.), 2012(3)ESC401(SC), 2012-4-LW567, 2012(5)SCALE702, (2012)7SCC683, [2012]114SCL441(SC), 2012(3)SLJ250(SC), MANU/SC/0496/2012

No. of pages in the Original Judgement: 8

Case Note:

FEMA - Legality of Order - Rules 2 (1) (b) and 5 of Foreign Exchange (Recruitment, Salary and Allowances and Other Conditions of Service of Chairperson and Members) Rules, 2000; Sections 20, 21, 21(1)(b), 21(2)(a) and 46 Foreign Exchange Management Act, 1999; Article 233 of Constitution of India, 1950 - High Court declared first and second proviso to Rule 5 of Rules, as ultra vires Section 21(1)(b) of Act, and quashed appointments of Respondent Nos. 3 and 4 who were appointed as part time Members and further quashed appointment of Respondent No. 3 as acting Chairperson of

Appellate Tribunal - Hence, present Appeals - Whether impugned order was illegal - Held, there was no conception of a part time Member under scheme of Act - A person, in order to be qualified for appointment as Chairperson, was required to be or had been qualified to be a Judge of High Court and a person to be a Member was required to be or had been qualified to be a district judge and to be appointed as a Special Director (Appeal), he had to be a member of the Indian Legal Service and was required to have held a post of Grade I or that service or a member of Indian Revenue Service as a post equivalent to Joint Secretary to Government of India - Thus, a member of Indian Legal Service who was qualified as per Section 21(2)(a) of Act, was entitled to be appointed as a Special Director (Appeal) - There were three distinctive forums for adjudication and there was a hierarchical system - Section 46 of Act, provided for rule making power - If a rule went beyond rule making power conferred by statute, then same had to be declared ultra vires - If a rule supplanted any provision for which power had not been conferred, it became ultra vires - Basic test was to determine and consider source of power which was relatable to rule - A rule must be in accord with parent statute as it could not travel beyond it - In case of Additional District Magistrate (Rev.) Delhi Administration v. Shri Ram, it had been ruled that, conferment of rule making power by an Act did not enable rule making authority to make a rule which traveled beyond scope of enabling Act or which was inconsistent therewith or repugnant thereto - Section 20 of Act, dealt with composition of Appellate Tribunal - Section 21 of Act, dealt with qualification for appointment of Chairperson, Member and Special Director (Appeals) - Appellate Tribunal had been conferred jurisdiction to decide an Appeal from Appellate Tribunal and it had to deal with matters relating to foreign exchange - If object and purpose of Act was to confer power on Appellate Board to deal with issue of economy under scheme of Act, it was well nigh impossible to conceive of appointment of a part time Member - Section 20 of Act, enabling provision, empowered Central Government to fix such number of persons as Government might deem fit - Main part of Rule 5 of Rules, provided that a tribunal would have one Chairperson and Members not exceeding four - To that extent, it was in consonance with Act and it came within framework of provision - First proviso stipulated that, number of either full time Members or part time Members would not exceed two - This proviso introduced concept of part time Member - It traveled beyond enabling provision and was totally inconsistent with it - Rule did not conform to main enactment - Therefore, High Court was justified in declaring said provision as ultra vires - Second proviso was an innovative one - It provided for qualification of a part time Member who could be appointed from amongst officers belonging to Indian Legal Service who fulfilled qualification prescribed under Clause (b) of Sub-Rule (1) of Rule 2 of Rules - Clause (b) of Sub-Rule (1) of Rule 2 of Rules, spelled out that a person would not be qualified for appointment as a Member unless, he was or had been or was qualified to be a district judge - Article 233 of Constitution, dealt with appointment of district judges - It provided for qualification to be a district judge - Rule 2 (1) (b) of Rules, provided qualification to be a Member - Same was in total accord with Act - First proviso to Rule 5 of Rules, introduced part time Member - Said proviso, as far as it introduced concept of part time Member, was contrary to provision contained in enabling Act - Section 46 of Act, nowhere envisaged about part time Members - Second proviso was an innovative one - There could not be a part time Member - A person who was qualified to be a district judge could be a Member if he met criterion laid down in pronouncements of this Court - They were strictly followed - There was no justification for introduction of second proviso to bring in officers from Indian Legal Service who were qualified to become district judges to be part time Members - If officer satisfied requisite qualification, he could be appointed as a Member - Therefore, second proviso had been incorporated to bring in only part time Members and once introduction of part time Members was treated to be ultra vires Act, rest part of Rule was redundant - If officer belonging to Indian Legal Services was qualified to be a district judge, he could compete and be selected for post of Member and that qualification was to be in accord with pronouncements of law of this Court - High Court had quashed appointment of part time Members and appointment of Chairperson who was a part time Member once - As appointment of part time Member was quashed, as a logical corollary, such a person could not be allowed to be appointed to post of Chairperson - Disqualified Member could not hold post of a Chairperson as a stop gap arrangement - Thus, there was no error in that regard in judgment passed by High Court - Appeals disposed

Brief facts of the case:

Calling in question the legal penetrability of the order dated April 12, 2004 passed by the Division Bench of the High Court of Judicature of Delhi in Writ Petition Nos. 7606 of 2003, 1335, 1336, 1337, 1344 and 1345 of 2004 by a common judgment, the present batch of appeals by way of special leave under Article 136 of the Constitution has been filed.

Though prayers in different writ petitions were couched differently, yet the three basic reliefs which were sought before the High Court are - Rule 5 of the Appellate Tribunal for Foreign Exchange (Recruitment, Salary and Allowances and Other Conditions of Service of Chairperson and Members) Rules, 2000 (hereinafter referred to as 'the Rules') is ultra vires the Foreign Exchange Management Act, 1999 (for brevity 'the Act); for quashment of certain notifications issued by the Government of India, Ministry of Law, Justice and Company Affairs, appointing part time Members of the Appellate Tribunal by issue of a writ of quo warranto as they did not satisfy the eligibility criteria as stipulated in the Act; and further to quash the appointment of Respondent No. 3 to act as the Chairperson as he was a part time Member and also was not eligible to hold the post.

Held,

We have referred to the aforesaid pronouncements to highlight who could be a person to be qualified to be a district judge. Rule 2 (1) (b) provides the qualification to be a Member. Needless to say, the same is in total accord with the Act. The first proviso to Rule 5 introduces part time Member. We have held that the said proviso, as far as it introduces the concept of part time Member, is contrary to the provision contained in the enabling Act. Section 46 of the Act nowhere envisages about the part time Members. The second proviso, we have already mentioned, is an innovative one. Thereafter, we have at length referred to the qualifications for a person to be a Member who is eligible to be a district judge. Once we have held that there cannot be a part time Member, a person who is qualified to be a district judge can be a Member if he meets the criterion laid down in the pronouncements of this Court. They are strictly followed. We really perceive no justification for the introduction of the second proviso to bring in officers from the Indian Legal Service who are qualified to become district judges to be part time Members. If the officer satisfies the requisite qualification, he can be appointed as a Member. Therefore, in our consideration, the second proviso has been incorporated to bring in only part time Members and once the introduction of part time Members is treated to be ultra vires the Act, the rest part of the Rule is absolutely redundant. To repeat at the cost of repetition, if the officer belonging to Indian Legal Services is qualified to be a district judge, he can compete and be selected for the post of Member and that qualification is to be in accord with the pronouncements of law of this Court.

The High Court, as we find, had quashed the appointment of part time Members and the appointment of Chairperson who was a part time Member once. As the appointment of part time Member was quashed, as a logical corollary, such a person could not be allowed to be appointed to the post of Chairperson. To elaborate; the disqualified Member cannot hold the post of a Chairperson as a stop gap arrangement. Thus, we do not find any error in that regard in the judgment passed by the High Court.

At this juncture, we are obliged to clarify the position further. This Court while issuing notice had granted stay on the operation of the judgment. We have been apprised by Mr. Bhatt that the Central Government, at present, has been scrupulously following the mandate of the Act and only qualified persons are appointed as Members and Chairperson. To avoid any confusion, we clarify that the judgments and orders passed by the Appellate Tribunal by the Chairperson or Members who were not qualified and whose appointments have been quashed shall not be treated to be null and void. In this regard we may refer with profit the decisions in ***Gokaraju Rangaraju v. State of Andhra Pradesh***MANU/SC/0143/1981 : AIR 1981 SC 1473 and ***M.M. Gupta and Ors. v. State of J. & K. and Ors.***MANU/SC/0033/1982 : AIR 1982 SC 1579 wherein this Court, while quashing the appointments of the Respondents, had clarified that the orders and judgments delivered by them during the period they had continued to function as district judges on the basis of invalid appointments could not be rendered as legally invalid and void. In the larger interest of justice, they are treated as valid and binding. Relying on the said dictum, we clarify the position accordingly.The appeals stand disposed of without any order as to costs.

ÞÞÞ

FOURTEEN

VIJAY KARIA AND ORS. VS. PRYSMIAN CAVI E SISTEMI SRL AND ORS., 2020

Hon'ble Judges/Coram: Rohinton Fali Nariman, Aniruddha Bose and V. Ramasubramanian, JJ.

Acts/Rules/Orders:

Arbitration (Protocol And Convention) Act, 1937 - Section 7(1); Arbitration And Conciliation Act, 1996 - Section 9, Section 28(3), Section 34, Section 34(2), Section 37, Section 45, Section 46, Section 47, Section 48, Section 48(1), Section 48(2), Section 49, Section 50, Section 75, Section 81; Conservation Of Foreign Exchange And Prevention Of Smuggling Activities Act, 1974 - Section 3; Constitution of India - Article 136, Article 142; Foreign Awards (recognition And Enforcement) Act, 1961 - Section 7, Section 7(1); Foreign Exchange Management (Non-Debt Instruments) Rules, 2019 - Rule 21, Rule 21(2); Foreign Exchange Regulation Act, 1973 - Section 47, Section 56; Foreign Exchange Management Act, 1999 Hong Kong Old Arbitration Ordinance - Section 23(2); London Court of International Arbitration Rules, 2014; Arbitration Act, 1996 (New York) - Section 100(2), Section 102(1), Section 103, Section 103(2), Section 103(3); International Arbitration Act - Section 13, Section 14, Section 19B(1), Section 24(b); Arbitration Act, 1996 (U.K.) - Section 68, Section 68(2), Section 70(2), Section 70(3), Section 73; Arbitration Act, 2002 (Singapore) - Section 48(1); Protocol and Convention Act, 1837 - Section

7(1); Federal Arbitration Act; Commercial Arbitration Act, 1984; United Nations Commission on International Trade Law Model Law on International Commercial Arbitration, 1985 - Article - 6, Article - 34, Article - 34(2), Article - 33(2); Arbitration and Conciliation (Amendment) Act, 2015

Equivalent Citation: AIR2020SC1807, 2020(1)ARBLR474(SC), (2020)11SCC1, 2020 (6) SCJ 144, MANU/SC/0171/2020

No. of pages in the Original Judgement: 42

Brief facts of the case:

The present appeals are filed against the judgment of a Single Judge of the Bombay High Court dated 07.01.2019, by which four final awards made by a sole arbitrator in London under the London Court of International Arbitration Rules (2014) (hereinafter referred to as the "LCIA Rules") were held to be enforceable against the Appellants in India.

3. The brief facts of this case are as follows. The Appellants, i.e. Appellant No. 1 Shri Vijay Karia, and Appellants No. 2 to 39 (who are represented by Appellant No. 1) are individual, non-corporate shareholders of Ravin Cables Limited (hereinafter referred to as "Ravin"). On 19.01.2010, the Appellants and Ravin entered into a Joint Venture Agreement (hereinafter referred to as "JVA") with Respondent No. 1, i.e. Prysmian Cavi E Sistemi SRL - a company registered under the laws of Italy. By this JVA, Respondent No. 1 acquired a majority shareholding (51%) of Ravin's share capital. The material clauses of the JVA are set out hereinbelow:

8. Purpose and Objectives

8.1 Purpose of the Company and Scope of the Agreement

Held,

The Respondents have also made a repeated reference to an allegation that the Tribunal lacked independence and that the Respondents have lost faith in the Tribunal continuing to give an impartial determination of the matters which remain in dispute.

These allegations have already been raised by the Respondents and rejected by the LCIA Court. Furthermore, the Respondents have not sought to invoke any procedure in the English Court, which is the court of the seat with supervisory jurisdiction. If the Respondents wished to challenge the ruling of the LCIA Court and challenge the further involvement of the Tribunal in the process, the Respondents had to bring a challenge within the strict time limits provided for in the English Arbitration Act 1996, but they have not done so. It is regretted that the Respondents continued to advance this unfounded and unparticularised allegation. The Tribunal has in the past pointed out the distinction between independence and impartiality on the one hand and on the other the role of an arbitrator who has to decide between rival arguments, diametrically opposed and irreconcilable positions adopted before it and direct clash of evidence before it and then apply such findings to the disputes before it. It is an inherent and an inevitable part of the arbitral process that where parties, as indeed has been the case in this arbitration, have taken radically opposing positions on the evidence and the law that multiple decisions will have to be made that will ultimately disappoint one of the parties. This has been exactly such a dispute. It has, however, been a distinct feature of this process that the Respondents have not only voiced their disappointment but have not complied with the orders of the Tribunal to protect the Parties' rights during the course of the Arbitration and not complied with the terms of the JVA as has been found and determined by the Tribunal in its prior Awards. In a dispute such as the present where it has been necessary to render a series of Awards, it is necessary for the Tribunal to apply the prior findings in any subsequent Award.

107. Having answered each of the submissions of Dr. Singhvi on behalf of the Appellants, we cannot help but be left with a feeling that the Appellants are indulging in a speculative litigation with the fond hope that by flinging mud on a foreign arbitral award, some of the mud so flung would stick. We have no doubt whatsoever that all the pleas taken by the Appellants are, in reality, pleas going to the unfairness of the conclusions reached by the award, which is plainly a foray into the merits of the matter, and which is plainly proscribed by Section 48 of the

FIFTEEN

Opera House Exports Ltd. Vs. Union of India (UOI), 2014

Hon'ble Judges/Coram: S.J. Mukhopadhaya and V. Gopala Gowda, JJ.

Subject: Criminal

Relevant Section:

Foreign Exchange Management Act, 1973 Section 51; Foreign Exchange Regulation Act, 1973 [Repealed] - Section 52

Equivalent Citation: 2014(141)AIC143, AIR2014SC3383, 2014(4)AJR706, 2014 (86) ACC 914, 2015 (2) ALT (Crl.) 412 (SC), 1(2015)CCR121(SC), [2015]125CLA28(SC), 2014CriLJ4154, 2014(146)DRJ15, 2015(315)ELT3(S.C.), 2014GLH(3)34, 2014(4)JCC2524, 2014(3)RCR(Criminal)871, 2014(8)SCALE547, (2014)12SCC610, 2015 (5) SCJ 332, MANU/SC/0637/2014

No. of pages in the Original Judgement: 42

Case Note:

Foreign Exchange Regulation Act, 1973 Sections 18, 33, 40 & 52(2) - Appeal - Limitation - Appeal against order under Section 51 can be filed within 45 days from the date on which the order is served on the person - Under Section 52 of FERA, Appellate Board was empowered to condone the delay - Impugned judgment and order passed by Tribunal and High Court set-aside - Appeals allowed.

Brief facts of the case:

The State Bank of India, Okhla Industrial Area, New Delhi by its XOS statement dated 21.01.1995 disclosed that the Appellant- M/s. Opera House Exports Ltd., D-12/2, Okhla Industrial Area, Phase-II, New Delhi (hereinafter referred to as the, 'Company') did not realize substantial amount of its export bills and that the bills pending realization were for the period 1991 to 1994. Since it was found that there was a prima facie case of violation of Section 18(2) & 18(3) of the FERA by the Company, the Respondent initiated inquiries against the Company with regard to the export bills pending realization, reasons for pendency and steps taken for realizing the said bills. During the course of investigation, a directive Under Section 33(2) of FERA was issued to the Company on 23.02.1996 in response to which the Company requested for time till 14.04.1996 for furnishing the requisite details. It was alleged that since no reply was furnished by the Company even by the said date summons was issued to the Directors of the Company on 16.05.1996, which also evoked no response from the Company. Summons was, therefore, issued to the Managing Director of the Company for his appearance on 10.09.1996. Since there was no compliance of the same, another summons was issued for his appearance on 30.09.1996. In response to the said summons, Mr. Sushil Kumar, Managing Director of the Company vide letter dated 28.09.1996, authorized Mrs. Rakesh Verma, General Manager (Finance) and Mr. Y.K. Jha, Manager (Export) to represent him in the matter. On 30.09.1996 Smt. Rakesh Verma, General Manager (Finance) attended the Directorate's Office and her statement was recorded Under Section 40 of the FERA. She explained the matter and also furnished copy of a letter dated 30.04.1996 from the State Bank of India (For short, 'SBI'), confirming realization of an amount of Rs. 9,72,203/- pertaining to the exports made during the period 1992-1995.

Held,

Therefore, we hold that even Under Section 52 of FERA the Appellate Board was empowered to condone the delay, as the appeal was filed before 90 days and not later than 90 days.

For the reasons aforesaid, we have no other option but to set aside the impugned judgment dated 9th February, 2011 passed by the High Court and the order dated 24th March, 2008 passed by the Tribunal. The case is remitted back to the Tribunal to decide the same on merit.

The appeals are allowed with aforesaid observations and directions. No costs.

PPP

SIXTEEN

RAM PARSHOTAM MITTAL AND ORS. VS. HOTEL QUEEN ROAD PVT. LTD. AND ORS. 2019

Hon'ble Judges/Coram:

Arun Mishra and Indira Banerjee, JJ.

Relevant Sections:

Foreign Exchange Management Act, 1999 - Section 6, Foreign Exchange Management Act, 1999 - Section 49, Foreign Exchange Regulation Act, 1973 [repealed] - Section 29, Section 29(1), Companies Act, 1956 - Section 108

Equivalent citations:

(2019)2015CompCas163(SC), 2019(5)CTC803, 2019(7)SCALE738, (2019)150CLA309(SC), MANU/SC/0741/2019

Case Notes:

Company - Allotment of shares - Voting rights - Sections 286, 300 and 108 of Companies Act, 1956 - Appeal arose out of judgment passed by High Court, setting aside an order passed by Company Law Board allowing appeal of Hillcrest and cancelled allotment and transfers made on 27th July, 2004, 7th January, 2005 and 10th May, 2005 on grounds that, Hillcrest had voting rights and there was breach of Sections 286, 300 and 108 of Companies Act - Whether there was breach of provisions of Companies Act.

Facts:

On 22nd August, 2005 Hillcrest and Ashok Mittal filed a petition under Sections 397 and 398 of the Companies Act alleging oppression and mis-management of HQRL by the R.P. Mittal Group. The Resolution passed in Board meetings regarding allotment/transfer of shares was also challenged on the ground that, no notice had been issued to Ashok Mittal who was, at the material time, a Director. The present case arises out of the said petition filed by Hillcrest and Mr. Ashok Mittal against the Appellants in the Company Law Board in September, 2005 under Sections 397/398 of the Act, challenging the allotment/transfer of shares effected on27th July, 2004, 7th January, 2005 and 10th May, 2005. It is alleged by the Appellants that, in spite of various hurdles created by Hilcrest and Mr. Ashok Mittal by sending notices to various Government departments asking them not to grant licenses, the hotel had become operational, with the sole efforts of Mr. R.P. Mittal. In August, 2006, Hilcrest filed a suit in High Court for a declaration that, Hilcrest had voting rights in HQRL in view of the Resolution dated 30th September, 2002 passed by HQRL. On 14th January, 2009, the Division Bench of Delhi High Court by a common order disposed of FAO upholding the right of Hilcrest to vote in the meetings of HQRL. Hilcrest took over the management of HQRL from R.P. Mittal Group through Ashok Mittal. On 30th July, 2009, Hilcrest and Ashok Mittal sent notice to the existing shareholders of HQRL under Section 81 (21) of the Companies Act to allot further equity shares. Appellants filed an interim application seeking injunction against Hilcrest and Mr. Ashok Mittal from going ahead with the rights issue. By a judgment, a Single Bench of Delhi High Court declined to interfere with the right issue and the application was dismissed. Appellant appealed against the order. The Division Bench, however, declined to restrain the rights issue but only directed issuance of notice to HQRL and Ashok Mittal. High Court by the impugned order allowed CoA (SB) 4/2006 of Hillcrest and cancelled the allotment and transfers on the grounds that, Hillcrest had voting rights and there was breach of Sections 286, 300 and 108 of the Companies Act.

Held, while disposing of the appeals

1. The Company Law Board as well as the High Court have found that, the provision of notice under Section 286 of the Companies Act was not complied with. The High Court has observed that, the interested Directors have participated in the meeting. Mr. R.P. Mittal and Mrs. Sarla Mittal were in a fiduciary capacity, they could not participate in the decision where

shares were transferred to their own group/company. Even if HQRL were a private limited company, the compliance with the provisions of Section 300 of the Act was mandatory. The High Court has also observed that, there was undervaluation of HQRL shares. The allotment of shares at par to Moral in the meeting on 10th May, 2005 and on the same very date, shares of Moral were transferred to Mr. R.P. Mittal @ Rs. 20 per share. Thus, the High Court has opined that, these acts in overall factual matrix of the case, were sufficient to conclude that ground under Section 397 had been made out. [66]

2. The High Court has also found that, HQRL did not have the share certificates along with duly executed share transfer forms when a decision was taken at the Board meeting held on 10th May, 2005 to transfer shares from Moral to Mr. R.P. Mittal. The decision has been held to be invalid for violation of provisions contained in Section 108 of the Act of 1956 for the aforesaid reason also. The Court has recorded suo motu proceedings under Section 340 of Code of Criminal Procedure against Mr. R.P. Mittal. The Court has invalidated the impugned resolutions dated 27th July, 2004, 7th January, 2005 and 10th May, 2005 and the decision of the Company Law Board has been set aside. [67]

3. The action taken as per the impugned resolutions were oppressive as they involved repeated violation of the mandatory provisions of the Companies Act of 1956 and was done surreptitiously without giving any notice to Mr. Ashok Mittal or Hillcrest. The attempt to convert the statutory status of HQRL vis-Ã -vis public company, Moral by transferring the shares of Moral in HQRL was against the interest of the preference shareholders of Hillcrest, therefore, it is oppressive. Hillcrest and Mr. Ashok Mittal have also supported the aforesaid submissions. [72]

4. In Needle Industries, it has been observed by this Court that, the resolution passed by the Director may be perfectly legal and yet oppressive and conversely a resolution which is in contravention of the law, may be in the interest of the shareholders of the company. Every illegality will not make it oppressive. Prejudice has to be shown. No complaint of oppression could be entertained merely on the ground of failure to attach notice of Board meeting was an act of illegality. It has to be shown that the action was unfair to the person to whom notice has not been given and causes prejudice to him in the exercise of legal and proprietary rights as shareholders. [75]

5. In Sangramsinh P. Gaekwad, it has been observed that their conduct is harsh, burdensome, wrong, mala fide or and is for a collateral purpose

against probity and good conduct. The impugned resolutions are unfair to Mr. Ashok Mittal in the facts and circumstances of the case even otherwise the absence of the notice is enough to invalidate the same as mandated by Section 286. [76]

6. It was improper for the Directors to allot shares to themselves and to the exclusion of Mr. Ashok Mittal in the facts and circumstances of the case and that too without issuance of notice to him. [81]

7. Section 19(2) of the Companies Act, provides that nothing in Sections 85 to 89 shall apply to a private company unless it is a subsidiary of a public company and this question has to be finally decided whether it is a private or public limited company in the pending civil suit which have been stated to be transferred to NCLT for decision in accordance with law. Otherwise, Section 87 provides that notice has to be issued to preference shareholders also for the meeting and they have a right to participate in the meeting. It appears prima facie even if dividend has not been declared. In that case also, preference shareholders shall have a right to vote in the meeting. [83]

8. Section 108 operates independently of Section 286 or Section 300. The invalidation of meeting is dependent under the provisions of Section 108. There was violation of Section 108 of the Companies Act. HQRL did not file share certificate along with the duly executed share transfer form as on 10th May, 2005, the date of Board resolution. The plea of Mr. R.P. Mittal has been disbelieved that share certificates were returned on 23rd June, 2003. The High Court has also ordered the proceedings under Section 340 of Code of Criminal Procedure against Mr. R.P. Mittal for filing an affidavit to the contrary. The High Court has relied on the affidavit of concerned officials of the Indian Overseas Bank. The High Court has found that the share certificates were delivered to Mr. R.P. Mittal not on 23rd June, 2003 but on 23rd June, 2005. [87]

9. The impugned order calls for no interference. However, direction to prosecute Appellant Ram Prakash Mittal in the facts of the case is set aside. [89]

10. The appeals are accordingly disposed of. [90]

SEVENTEEN

M. Umesh Vs. Assistant Director, Directorate of Enforcement, 2021

Hon'ble Judges/Coram: A.M. Khanwilkar and Sanjiv Khanna, JJ.

Acts/Rules/Orders:

Foreign Exchange Management Act

Equivalent Citation: 2021(377)ELT787(S.C.), MANU/SC/0774/2021

No. of pages in the Original Judgement: 2

Brief facts of the case:

SLP(C) No(s). 18534/2019: This special leave petition is directed against the judgment of the High Court taking the view that the Petitioner must avail of the statutory remedy, as the competent authority has passed final order on 31-1-2019.

We agree with the view so taken by the High Court.

Mr. Mukul Rohatgi, learned Senior Counsel appearing for the Petitioner would submit that the Petitioner was in no way concerned with the affairs of the company after his resignation on 6-5-2006 much less with the agreement dated 21-6-2006. Further, even the earlier agreement was between the two companies to which the Petitioner was not a signatory.

Held,

Accordingly, we dispose of this petition with liberty to the Petitioner to file statutory appeal within three weeks from today.

If the appeal is filed in time, as aforesaid, the Appellate Authority may proceed with the appeal on its own merits in accordance with law and not non-suit this Petitioner on ground of limitation as the Petitioner has been bona fide pursuing remedy against the show cause first before the High Court and also before this Court.

It will be open to the Petitioner to file a formal application before the Appellate Authority for granting exemption from paying 100% pre-deposit amount. That application be considered on its own merits and in accordance with law. We may not be understood to have expressed any view either way in that regard.

If the appeal is not filed within three weeks from today, the limited relief given to the Petitioner with regard to period of limitation may stand withdrawn and the appeal may proceed accordingly.

Pending applications, if any, stand disposed of.

EIGHTEEN

SHAILENDRA SWARUP VS. THE DEPUTY DIRECTOR, ENFORCEMENT DIRECTORATE, 2014

Hon'ble Judges/Coram: Ashok Bhushan and R. Subhash Reddy, JJ.

Acts/Rules/Orders:

Adjudication Proceedings & Appeal Rules, 1974 - Rule 3; Companies Act, 1956 - Section 291; Foreign Exchange Management Act, 1999 - Section 3, Section 4, Section 49; Foreign Exchange Regulation Act, 1973 - Section 8(3), Section 8(4), Section 50, Section 51, Section 68, Section 68(1); Negotiable Instruments Act, 1881 - Section 138, Section 141, Section 141(1), Section 141(2), Section 142

Equivalent Citation: AIR2020SC3890, 2020 (3) ALT (Crl.) 78 (A.P.), 2020(5)BLJ244, 2020(3)BomCR(Cri)88, [2020]159CLA12(SC), [2020]221CompCas758(SC), 2020(2)Crimes369(SC), 2020(373)ELT433(S.C.), 2021-1-LW(Crl)9, 2020(3)MLJ(Crl)721, 2020(3)RCR(Criminal)138, (2020)16SCC561, 2020 (6) SCJ 696, [2020]161SCL1(SC), MANU/SC/0544/2020

No. of pages in the Original Judgement: 11

Case Note:

FERA - Penalty - Deletion of - Sections 3,4,8(3), 8(4),49, 68 and 51 of Foreign Exchange Regulation Act, 1973 - Remittances were made by one company through its banker - Enforcement Directorate wrote to company for supplying invoices as well as purchase orders - Company provided for four transactions and Chartered Accountant's Certificates for balance amounts - Show cause notice was issued by Deputy Director, Enforcement Directorate to company and its Directors, including Appellant - Show cause notice required to show cause in writing as to why adjudication proceedings as contemplated in Section 51 of Act should not be held for contravention - Company replied show cause notice - Directorate of Enforcement decided to hold proceedings as contemplated in Section 51 of Act read with Section 3 and 4 of Section 49 of Act - Deputy Director imposed penalty on Appellant for contravention of Section 8(3) read with 8(4) and Section 68 of Act - Aggrieved by order of imposing penalty on Appellant, appeal was filed by Appellant before Appellate Tribunal which was dismissed - Against order of Appellate Tribunal, appeal was filed in High Court which also dismissed - Hence, present appeal - Whether penalty on Appellant for contravention of Section 8(3) read with 8(4) and Section 68 of Act was sustainable.

Brief facts of the case:

The remittances were made by the one Company through its banker Standard Chartered Bank. The Reserve Bank of India issued a letter stating that despite reminder issued by the Authorised Dealer, company had not submitted the Exchange Control copy of the custom bills of Entry/Postal Wrappers as evidence of import of goods into India. Enforcement Directorate wrote to company for supplying invoices as well as purchase orders. Company provided for four transactions and Chartered Accountant's Certificates for balance amounts for which company's Bankers were unable to trace old records. A show cause notice was issued by the Deputy Director, Enforcement Directorate to company and its Directors, including the Appellant. The show cause notice required to show cause in writing as to why adjudication proceedings as contemplated in Section 51 of Foreign Exchange Regulation Act, 1973 should not be held for contravention. The Directorate of Enforcement decided to hold proceedings as contemplated in Section 51 of the FERA, 1973 read with Section 3 and 4 of Section 49 of FEMA. In the reply the Appellant stated that he is a practicing Advocate of the Supreme Court and was only a part-time, non-executive Director of company and he was never in the employment of the Company nor had executive role in the functions of the Company. It was further stated that the Appellant was never in charge of nor ever responsible for the conduct of business of the Company. Along with the reply an affidavit of the Company Secretary that the Appellant who was the Director of erstwhile Company was only a part-time, Director of the said Company and never in charge of day to day business of the Company was also filed. The Deputy Director, Enforcement Directorate after hearing the Appellant, other Directors of the Company passed an order imposing a penalty on the Appellant for contravention of Section 8(3) read with 8(4) and Section 68 of FERA, 1973. Aggrieved by the order imposing penalty on the Appellant, appeal was filed by the Appellant before the Appellate Tribunal for Foreign Exchange which appeal came to be dismissed by the Appellate Tribunal. Against the order of the Appellate Tribunal, appeal was filed by the Appellant in High Court. The High Court by the impugned judgment had dismissed the appeal of the Appellant.

Held,

It is also relevant to notice that an order which was passed on 13.02.2004 by the Deputy Director in adjudication proceedings although with regard to different period, the plea of the Appellant that he was only a part-time, non-executive Director and not responsible of the conduct of business of the Company was accepted and notice was discharged against the Appellant. The order dated 13.02.2004 although related to different period but has categorically noticed the status of the Appellant as part-time non-executive Director. There being decision of Adjudicating Authority, in the recent past, passed on 13.02.2004, that the Appellant was only a part-time non-executive Director of MXL, there has to be some reasons for taking a contrary view by the adjudicating officer in order dated 31.03.2004 with regard to affairs of the same company, i.e., MXL.

In view of the foregoing discussions, we are of the view that the adjudicating officer has erroneously imposed penalty on the Appellant for the alleged offence Under Section 8(3), 8(4) and 68 of the FERA, 1973 which order was erroneously affirmed both by the Appellate Tribunal and the High Court.

In view of the aforesaid, this appeal deserves to be allowed, the judgments of the High Court as well as those of the adjudicating officer and the Appellate Tribunal are set aside. The appeal is allowed and the penalty imposed on the Appellant is set aside.

❧❧❧

NINETEEN

DIRECTOR OF INCOME TAX-II (INTERNATIONAL TAXATION), NEW DELHI AND ORS. VS. SAMSUNG HEAVY INDUSTRIES CO. LTD., 2020

Hon'ble Judges/Coram: Rohinton Fali Nariman, Navin Sinha and B.R. Gavai, JJ.

Acts/Rules/Orders:

Foreign Exchange Management (Establishment in India of Branch or Office or other place of business) (Amendment) Regulations 2003; Income-tax Act, 1961 - Section 4(2), Section 9, Section 90, Section 90(2)

Equivalent Citation: AIR2020SC3906, (2020)315CTR(SC)622, [2020]426ITR1(SC), (2020)6MLJ81, (2020)7SCC347, [2020]272TAXMAN377(SC), MANU/SC/0534/2020

No. of pages in the Original Judgement: 9

Case Note:

Direct Taxation - Taxability of income - Assessment Year 2007-2008 - Permanent Establishment - Agreement for avoidance of double taxation of income and the prevention of fiscal evasion' with the Republic of Korea - Article 5 thereof - Whether maintenance of a fixed place of business of a preparatory or auxiliary character in the trade or business of the enterprise, not to be considered to be a permanent establishment?

Brief Facts of the case:

Oil and Natural Gas Company (ONGC) awarded a "turnkey" contract to a consortium comprising of the Respondent/Assessee (a Company incorporated in South Korea), and Larsen & Toubro Limited, being a contract for carrying out the "Work", inter alia, of surveys, design, engineering, procurement, fabrication, installation and modification at existing facilities, and start-up and commissioning of entire facilities covered under the 'Vasai East Development Project' ("Project").Assessee later set up a Project Office in Mumbai, India, which, as per the Assessee, was to act as "a communication channel" between the Assessee and ONGC in respect of the Project. Pre-engineering, survey, engineering, procurement and fabrication activities which took place abroad, all took place in the year 2006. Commencing from November, 2007, these platforms were then brought outside Mumbai to be installed at the Vasai East Development Project, to be completed by 26.07.2009. With regard to Assessment Year 2007-2008, Assessee filed a Return of Income showing nil profit and sufferance of loss allegedly been incurred in relation to the activities carried out by it in India. A show-cause notice was issued to the Assessee requiring it to show cause as to why the Return of Income had been filed only at nil, which was replied to in detail by the Assessee. A draft Assessment Order was then passed and concluded that the Project in question was a single indivisible "turnkey" project, whereby ONGC was to take over a project that is completed only in India. Resultantly, profits arising from the successful commissioning of the Project would also arise only in India. The Draft Order then went on to attribute 25% of the revenues allegedly earned outside India as being the income of the Assessee exigible to tax. The Dispute Resolution Panel after considering objections to the Draft Order by the Assessee held that the AO had given a specific finding that the Assessee had a project office in India, when it was given the contract. The Assessee did not contested the existence of the Project office in India. It only contested that the project was used merely for preparatory and auxiliary activities. This submission of the

Assessee was not accepted. The Draft Order was made final that lead to filing of appeal against the Assessment Order before the ITAT, which confirmed the findings of AO and Dispute Resolution Panel. High Court in appeal held that the question as to whether the Project Office opened at Mumbai could not be said to be a "permanent establishment" within the meaning of Article 5 of the DTAA would be of no consequence. It held that there was no finding that 25% of the gross revenue of the Assessee outside India was attributable to the business carried out by the Project Office of the Assessee. According to the High Court, neither the Assessing Officer nor the ITAT made any effort to bring on record any evidence to justify this figure. Appeal of the Assessee was accordingly allowed. Hence, the present appeal.

Held,

A reading of the Board Resolution would show that the Project Office was established to coordinate and execute "delivery documents in connection with construction of offshore platform modification of existing facilities for ONGC". Unfortunately, the ITAT relied upon only the first paragraph of the Board Resolution, and then jumped to the conclusion that the Mumbai office was for coordination and execution of the project itself. The finding, therefore, that the Mumbai office was not a mere liaison office, but was involved in the core activity of execution of the project itself is therefore clearly perverse. Equally, when it was pointed out that the accounts of the Mumbai office showed that no expenditure relating to the execution of the contract was incurred, the ITAT rejected the argument, stating that as accounts are in the hands of the Assessee, the mere mode of maintaining accounts alone cannot determine the character of permanent establishment. This is another perverse finding which is set aside. Equally the finding that the onus is on the Assessee and not on the Tax Authorities to first show that the project office at Mumbai is a permanent establishment is again in the teeth of our judgment in E-Funds IT Solution Inc. (supra).

Though it was pointed out to the ITAT that there were only two persons working in the Mumbai office, neither of whom was qualified to perform any core activity of the Assessee, the ITAT chose to ignore the same. This being the case, it is clear, therefore, that no permanent establishment has been set up within the meaning of Article 5(1) of the DTAA, as the Mumbai Project Office cannot be said to be a fixed place of business through which the core business of the Assessee was wholly or partly carried on. Also, as correctly argued by Shri Ganesh, the Mumbai Project Office, on the facts of the present case, would fall within Article 5(4)(e) of the DTAA, inasmuch as the office is solely an auxiliary office, meant to act as a liaison office between the Assessee and ONGC. This being the case, it is not necessary to go into any of the other questions that have been argued before us.

The appeal against the impugned High Court judgment is therefore dismissed, but for the reasons stated by us.

TWENTY

SUBORNO BOSE VS. ENFORCEMENT DIRECTORATE AND ORS., 2020

Hon'ble Judges/Coram: A.M. Khanwilkar and Dinesh Maheshwari, JJ.

Relevant Section:

Foreign Exchange Management Act, 1999 - Section 42(1)

Equivalent Citation: AIR2020SC4288, [2020]159CLA1(SC), 2020(372)ELT3(S.C.), (2020)2MLJ646, (2020)14SCC241, [2020]160SCL607(SC), MANU/SC/0285/2020

No. of pages in the Original Judgement: 7

Case Note:

FEMA - Penalty - Determination of liability - Sections 10(6), 42(1), 46 and 47 of Foreign Exchange Management Act, 1999 - Show cause notice was issued to Appellant, stating that Adjudicating Authority was satisfied that there was prima facie contravention of Section 10(6) of FEMA Act read with Sections 46 and 47 of said Act - Reply to show-cause notice filed on behalf of Company including for Appellant - Adjudicating Authority concluded that noticee Company and Appellant had violated Section 10(6) of FEMA Act read with Sections 46 and 47 of Act having found that goods had arrived in India, but Company failed to submit Bill of Entry and did not take delivery of goods - Resultantly, Adjudicating Authority imposed penalty on Appellant and noticee company - Company, as well as, Appellant filed appeals before

Appellate authority - Appellate Authority dismissed appeals and was pleased to uphold decision of Adjudicating Authority - Being aggrieved, Company, as well as Appellant carried matter before High Court - Both appeals were dismissed by High Court - Hence, present appeal - Whether Appellant could be made liable for contravention committed by erstwhile management of Company.

Brief Facts of the case:

A show-cause notice was issued to the Appellant, stating that the Adjudicating Authority was satisfied that there was a prima facie contravention of Section 10(6) of the FEMA Act read with Sections 46 and 47 of the said Act and the Foreign Exchange Manual in the complaint filed against the company of which, the Appellant was the Managing Director. The reply to the show-cause notice filed on behalf of the Company including for the Appellant and the submissions made before the Adjudicating Authority were duly considered by the Adjudicating Authority. The Adjudicating Authority concluded that the noticee Company and the Appellant had violated the provisions of Section 10(6) of the FEMA Act read with Sections 46 and 47 of the said Act read with the Foreign Exchange Manual having found that the goods had arrived in India, but the Company failed to submit Bill of Entry and did not take delivery of the goods. The import formalities would have had completed only after submission of Bill of Entry. Thus, though the goods for which foreign exchange was remitted had reached the destination of the users, but the same were not released and as such kept in bonded warehouse. That resulted in contravention warranting issuance of show-cause notice to the Company and the Appellant. Resultantly, the Adjudicating Authority imposed penalty on Appellant and the company. The Company, as well as, the Appellant carried the matter in appeal before the Special Director (Appeals), FEMA and Commissioner of Income-Tax. The Appellate Authority dismissed both the appeals and was pleased to uphold the decision of the Adjudicating Authority. Being aggrieved, the Company, as well as the Appellant carried the matter before the High Court. Both appeals were dismissed by the High Court.

Held,

The Tribunal has erroneously relied on the judgment in *Hindustan Steel Ltd. v. State of Orissa*, MANU/SC/0418/1969 : (1969) 2 SCC 627 which pertained to criminal/quasi-criminal proceedings. That Section 25 of the Orissa Sales Tax Act which was in question in the said case imposed a punishment of imprisonment up to six months and fine for the offences under the Act. The said case has no application in the present case which relates to imposition of civil liabilities under the SEBI Act and the Regulations and is not a criminal/quasi-criminal proceeding.

We are in agreement with the view so expressed.

To sum up, we hold that no error has been committed by the adjudicating authority in finding that the Appellant was also liable to be proceeded with for the contravention by the Company of which he became the Managing Director and for penalty therefor as prescribed for the contravention of Section 10(6) read with Sections 46 and 47 of the FEMA Act read with paragraphs A-10 and A-11 (Current Account Transaction) of the Foreign Exchange Manual 2003-04. The first appellate authority and the High Court justly affirmed the view so taken by the adjudicating authority.

Accordingly, this appeal fails and the same is dismissed with no order as to costs.

Videos & Tv Shows On Law & Exim

List of some important videos & TV shows on Law & EXIM by Adv. Jayprakash Somani on his YouTube Channel 'Jayprakash Somani EXIM & Legal'

Legal Videos: Hindi -English

1) SLP in Supreme Court / Special Leave Petitions in the Supreme Court of India

2) Transfer of Civil & Criminal Cases by the Supreme Court of India / Transfer of Matrimonial Cases

3) Appellate Jurisdiction of the Supreme Court of India

4) Jurisdictions of the Supreme Court of India

5) Public Interest Litigation in the Supreme Court of India / PIL in Supreme Court

6) Article 32 Writ Petitions in the Supreme Court of India

7) Bail Matters Top 10 Supreme Court Cases

8) FIR Quashing in High Court & Supreme Court

9) Bail & Anticipatory Bail Matters in Supreme Court

10) Insolvency & Bankruptcy Matters in the Supreme Court

11) Insolvency & Bankruptcy Code 2016 Part 1

12) Insolvency & Bankruptcy Code 2016 Part 2

13) Insolvency & Bankruptcy Code 2016 Part 3

14) Corporate Liquidation Process

15) Supreme Court Rules & Procedures Webinar of 2.5 hour on Zoom

16) RDDBFI Act, 1993 (Introduction)

17) The Indian Contact Act 1872

18) Negotiable Instruments Act (Introduction)

19) How to avoid matrimonial disputes& some more videos

20)SEBI Matters in the Supreme Court

21) Matrimonial Matters: Supreme Court's 20 Case Laws

22) Consumer Matters Supreme Court's 20 Case Laws

23) Service Matters Supreme Court's 20 Case Laws

24) How to Search Lawyer for Your Matter

25) Property Matters Supreme Court's 20 Case Laws

26) Bail Matters: Supreme Court's 20 Case Laws

27) Supreme Court / High Court Vacation Benches

28)69000 Teacher's Recruitment Matters of UP Government in the Supreme Court

29) Contempt of Court Matters in the Supreme Court

30) Advocate Act's Matters in the Supreme Court

31) Business Law Matters in the Supreme Court

32) Banking Matters in the Supreme Court

33) Labour Law Matters in the Supreme Court

34) Arbitration Matters in the Supreme Court

35) Careers in Law -Zoom Webinar by Adv. Jayprakash Somani

36) Civil Matters in the Supreme Court

37) Consumer Protection Act | Consumer Matters in the Supreme Court

38) Corporate Matters in the Supreme Court

39) Criminal Matters in the Supreme Court

40) Role of Respondent in the Supreme Court of India

41) Motor Vehicle Accident Matters in Supreme Court with case laws

42) Article 131 Original Suits in Supreme Court

43)PIL in Supreme Court/ Public Interest Litigations in the Supreme Court of India'

44)CAB Citizenship Amendment Bill is not Unconstitutional

45) Supreme Court of India Cases & Process – Marathi

46) Legal Services Export / Export of Legal Services

47) Transfer of Matrimonial Cases by the Supreme Court of India

48) Public Interest Litigation PIL

49) The Specific Relief Act (Introduction)

50) Corporate Insolvency Resolution Process CIRP

51)ABMM's Career 5 - Careers in Law

52) Transfer of cases by Supreme Court

53) Writ Petitions in High Court & Supreme Court of India

54) Supreme Court Jurisdictions - Appeals, SLP, Writ Petitions, Transfer, Original, Review, Curative

55)LEGAL INDIA TV Show: Cases Handled in Supreme Court

56) Corporate Liquidation Process

57) Legal Services Export / Export of Legal Services

EXIM Videos: Hindi -English

1) Yes, I can do Import Export Business Easily! 36 points excellent video in Hindi

2) Yes, I can do Import Export Business Easily! 36 points excellent video in English

3) Import Export Business – Hindi video

4) Import Export Business - English video

5) Export Import Marathi TV Interview

6) Scope for Commerce Students in International Business- TV Show

7) Scope for Management Student in International Business- TV Show

8) Scope for Engineering Students in International Business – TV Show

9) Women in International Business- TV Show

10) How to do Import Export Business Successfully!'

11) Where one can get full information on Import Export Business?

12) What to do import & export?

13) Import Export Workshop/ Training/Course/ Diploma

14) How to Start Import Export Business & How to grow it. Live Webinar

15) Success Stories & Failure Stories in Import & Export Business

16) For MSME Scope in Export & Import...

17) Exports In Agri. & Food Products – English & some more videos

18) Exports to Dubai, Aabudhabii. e. UAE

19) Jewellery Exports from India

20) How to attend EXIM workshop to become excellent Exporter

21) Import Export Best Training Course – Online & Offline

22) Agri Product Export

23) Scope for Woman in International Business

24) Management Graduates Scope in International Business

25) Pharma Product's Export

26) Best Import Export Course | Practical Training | Aaronica Global Exim

27) Import Export Business for Commerce Graduates

28) How Do I Get Export Orders? Finding International Buyers

29) What Is APEDA In Import Export Business?

30) Which Is The Best Product To Export From India?

31)EXIM Remark by Manoj Kumar Faridabad

32)EXIM Remarks by Mahesh Telangana

33) What Licenses I Need To Start Import/ Export?

34) How Can I Increase My Import Export Business?

35) Which Is Best B2B Website For Import/Export Business?

36) Export Import Management with Global Marketing

37) How to Start Export Import Business | 51 Points Video

38) Scope for Commerce & Other Graduates in International Business

39)BE A SUCCESSFUL EXPORTER FOR OUR NATION - Marathi video

40) Export of Textile , Cotton, Agri., Food, & other products & services

41) Exports from MP, CG, MH, GJ & CA in Fresh Fruits & Vegetables

42) Exports in Agri. & Food Products- Hindi

43) Start your Online/E-Commerce Business

44) How to Start Export Import Business & Grow it

45) Exports in Textile & Other Products

46) Start and grow EXIM business - Live English Webinar

47)'Import Export Business!' Why, Who, What & How can one do it easily!!

48) Live: Export of Product & Services During & After Lock Down Period

49) Frauds in Import Export Business

50) Import Export for Business Man

51) Import & Export for Women

51) Import & Export for Graduate & Post - Graduate Students

52) Agriculture Exports from India

53) Digital Marketing Setup - Marathi

54)2nd Secret of Successful Businessman

55) Digital Marketing Set up

56) Legal Services Export / Export of Legal Services

57) Export & Import with UAE

58) Service Exports / Exports by Service Providers

59) Import Export Workshop/ Training/Course/ Diploma

60) Exports & Imports with USA

61) Selection on Product for Export

62) Top Products Exported from India

63) What to do import & export?

64)ABMM Career 2 - 'Careers in Business & Industries

65) How to do Import Export Business Successfully!'

66)5 Secrets of Successful Businessman

67) Export from MP, Chhattisgarh & Vidarbha Nagpur

68)EXIM Hindi - Textile & Apparel Export

69)EXIM Hindi - Export Import Practical Training In Delhi, Kolkata, Mumbai and Pune

70) Import Export Business

71) Import Export Business Hindi

72) Import Export Business English video

73) Import Export Business Marathi

74) Women in International Business by Exim Guru Adv. Jayprakash Somani

75) Opportunities in Foreign Trade- Adv. Jayprakash Somani's special interview

❦❦❦

List Of Adv. Jayprakash Somani's Books

1. Supreme Court of India's Leading Case Laws on 'Insolvency & Bankruptcy Code 2016'
2. Bail Matters – Supreme Court's Latest Leading Case Laws
3. Arbitration Matters- Supreme Court's Latest Leading Case Laws
4. Property Matters - Supreme Court's Latest Leading Case Laws
5. Matrimonial Matters- Supreme Court's Latest Leading Case Laws
6. Election Matters- Supreme Court's Latest Leading Case Laws
7.SEBI Matters- Supreme Court's Latest Leading Case Laws
8. Banking Matters- Supreme Court's Latest Leading Case Laws
9. Service Matters- Supreme Court's Latest Leading Case Laws
10. Contempt of Court Matters- Supreme Court's Latest Leading Case Laws
11. Consumer Protection Matters- Supreme Court's Latest Leading Case Laws
12. Corporate Law- Supreme Court's Latest Leading Case Laws
13. Supreme Court's AOR Exam- Leading Cases
14. Armed Force Tribunal - Supreme Court's Latest Leading Case Laws
15. Acquittal From 376 - Supreme Court's Latest Leading Case Laws
16. Negotiable instrument – Supreme Court's Latest Leading Case Laws
17. Contract Act- Supreme Court's Latest Leading Case Laws
18. Insider trading- Supreme Court's Latest Leading Case Laws
19. Foreign Exchange and Management Act- Supreme Court's Latest Leading Case Laws
20. Income Tax Act- Supreme Court's Latest Leading Case Laws
21. Company Law- Supreme Court's Latest Leading Case Laws
22. Competition & Monopoly Matters- Supreme Court's Latest Leading Case Laws
23. Compassionate Appointment- Service Matters- Supreme Court's Latest Leading Case Laws
24. Compulsory Retirement- Service Matters- Supreme Court's Latest Leading Case Laws
25. Voluntary Retirement- Service Matters- Supreme Court's Latest Leading Case Laws
26. Removal/Dismissal/Termination from Service- Supreme Court's Latest Leading Case Laws

27. Seniority- Service Matter- Supreme Court's Latest Leading Case Laws

28. Promotion- Service Matter- Supreme Court's Latest Leading Case Laws

29. Equal Pay for Equal Work- Service Matter- Supreme Court's Latest Leading Case Laws

30. Condition of Service- Service Matter- Supreme Court's Latest Leading Case Laws

31. Customs Act- Supreme Court's Leading Case Laws

ᑭᑭᑭ

These Books are available online at

1. **Notion Press:** https://notionpress.com/author/jayprakash_somani
2. **Amazon:** https://www.amazon.in/s?k=jayprakash+somani
3. **Flipkart:** https://www.flipkart.com/search?q=Jayprakash%20Somani

ᑭᑭᑭ

9 798885 917063

Printed by Libri Plureos GmbH in Hamburg,
Germany